Health & Wellbeing 1
PSHE IN SCOTLAND

Health & Wellbeing 1

PSHE IN SCOTLAND

Marel Harper, Gail Whitnall
Lesley de Meza & Stephen De Silva

Hachette UK's policy is to use papers that are natural, renewable and recyclable products and made from wood grown in sustainable forests. The logging and manufacturing processes are expected to conform to the environmental regulations of the country of origin.

Orders: please contact Bookpoint Ltd, 130 Milton Park, Abingdon, Oxon OX14 4SB. Telephone: (44) 01235 827720. Fax: (44) 01235 400454. Lines are open 9.00–5.00, Monday to Saturday, with a 24-hour message answering service. Visit our website at www.hoddereducation.co.uk. Hodder Gibson can be contacted direct on: Tel: 0141 848 1609; Fax: 0141 889 6315; email: hoddergibson@hodder.co.uk

© Lesley de Meza, Stephen De Silva, Gail Whitnall and Marel Harper (2008) 2010

First published as *PSHE Education 1* by Lesley de Meza and Stephen De Silva in 2008 by
Hodder Education,
An Hachette UK Company
338 Euston Road
London NW1 3BH

This edition first published 2010 by
Hodder Gibson, an imprint of Hodder Education,
An Hachette UK Company
2a Christie Street
Paisley PA1 1NB

Impression number   5 4 3 2 1
Year   2012 2011 2010

All rights reserved. Apart from any use permitted under UK copyright law, no part of this publication may be reproduced or transmitted in any form or by any means, electronic or mechanical, including photocopying and recording, or held within any information storage and retrieval system, without permission in writing from the publisher or under licence from the Copyright Licensing Agency Limited. Further details of such licences (for reprographic reproduction) may be obtained from the Copyright Licensing Agency Limited, Saffron House, 6–10 Kirby Street, London EC1N 8TS.

Cover photo © Relaximages/Alamy
Illustrations by Richard Duszczak, and Oxford Designers and Illustrators
Typeset in 12pt Avenir by Fakenham Photosetting Limited, Fakenham, Norfolk
Printed and bound in Italy

A catalogue record for this title is available from the British Library

ISBN: 978 1444 112 740

About the authors

Gail Whitnall and Marel Harper

Gail Whitnall and Marel Harper were seconded together as part of a team supporting the development of Curriculum for Excellence (CfE) for Renfrewshire Council during 2008–2009.

Gail has worked in secondary education for 10 years with 6 years of experience as Principal Teacher of a successful Health, Food and Technology department and is an SQA verifier for certificated PSE. Her seconded role was Health and Wellbeing Development Officer through which she promoted effective partnership working and the sharing of good practice and also supported the development of whole school policy and practice.

Marel has worked in primary education for 16 years. Having spent three years as Principal Teacher with responsibility for Expressive Arts, Physical Education and supporting the development of Health and Wellbeing, Marel was seconded as Renfrewshire Council's Curriculum for Excellence Development Officer. Through this post Marel has been involved in a variety of projects developing all aspects of CfE with a focus on effective learning and teaching, embedding Assessment is for Learning practice, interdisciplinary learning and promoting professional dialogue, and the sharing of good practice as key aspects of continuing professional development.

Together, Gail and Marel have collaborated on a number of local and national initiatives which contribute to the support provided for schools and local authorities in the implementation of Health and Wellbeing within Curriculum for Excellence.

Stephen De Silva

Stephen is an experienced trainer, assessor, consultant and writer with 30 years' service in the public sector. He has worked across the UK and in the USA, Bermuda and Taiwan. Originally a leader of both PSHE/Religious Education departments and Pastoral Year Teams, he has also managed young people's sexual health and drugs services in the NHS.

Stephen has been:
- a contributor to Teachers' TV programmes
- a consultant to QCA on the Personal Development curriculum review
- an associate trainer for the National Children's Bureau
- a writer and trainer on the Home Office's 'Blueprint' Drugs Project
- an accredited trainer of SHARE (Sexual Health and Relationships Education) for NHS Scotland.

He works with the subject of Diversity (particularly looking at topics such as sexuality and religious/cultural awareness) and provides training skills development for those working in Safeguarding Children (Child Protection). His voluntary work includes his role as Cathedral Warden and Honorary Canon at St. Albans Abbey.

Lesley de Meza

Lesley is a leading practitioner, trainer and writer known internationally for her PSHE education work. In England she worked as part of a QCA project team on Personal and Social Development curriculum materials and case studies. She also works with a range of organisations including DAATs, DCSF, DoH, HIT (Liverpool), Home Office, Integrated Youth Support Services, LAs, Metropolitan Police, NICE, PCTs, QCDA, schools, TPU and universities.

Lesley serves as an 'Educational Practitioner' member of the Public Health Interventions Advisory Committee (PHIAC), which is part of the National Institute for Health & Clinical Excellence (NICE). She is an Associate Trainer for the National Children's Bureau and Brook and also a Trustee for JAT (Jewish Action and Training for Sexual Health).

Contents

CHAPTER 1 Starting out
  1 What is PSHE?   4
  2 How will we work together?   6
  3 Where are we going?   8

CHAPTER 2 Healthy routines
  4 What do we need to do to keep healthy?   10
  5 What is my personal health profile?   12
  6 What decisions can I make about healthy eating?   14

CHAPTER 3 Substance misuse
  7 What do we mean by 'drugs'?   16
  8 Fact or fiction?   18
  9 How do we reduce the risks?   20
  10 How do drugs affect people?   22

CHAPTER 4 Relationships, sexual health and parenthood
  11 What do we mean by 'family'?   24
  12 Is commitment important in relationships?   26
  13 How can we contribute to family life?   28
  14 What's happening to me?   30
  15 Why do I feel like this?   32

CHAPTER 5 Assessing risk
  16 How do we manage risky situations?   34
  17 How do we keep safe online?   36
  18 How can we tackle bullying?   38

CHAPTER 6 Meeting and working with others
19 How do I work best with others? — 40
20 What do I want and how do I get it? — 42
21 What do I do if I need help? — 44

CHAPTER 7 Managing personal money
22 What could we do with money? — 46
23 Do I spend or do I save money? — 48
24 How will I earn money in the future? — 50

CHAPTER 8 Changing
25 What are my rights and responsibilities? — 52
26 What makes each of us an individual? — 54
27 How can I make and keep good relationships? — 56

CHAPTER 9 Personal identity and self-esteem
28 Who am I? — 58
29 What am I good at? — 60
30 Where am I going? — 62

CHAPTER 10 Confident communication
31 How can we communicate better? — 64
32 What does 'assertiveness' mean? — 66
33 What are the biggest challenges for me? — 68

CHAPTER 11 Review
34 Hey, how are you doing? — 70

Index — 74

Starting out 1

What is PSHE?

In this lesson you will learn:
★ what PSHE is all about.

Get Active 1

Think back to when you were in Primary 7. What did you enjoy, what were you looking forward to, and what did you worry about? In small groups divide a large piece of paper into four sections with the headings:

1. We were worried about …
2. Outside school we enjoyed …
3. In school we enjoyed …
4. We were looking forward to …

Fill in the sections with your ideas. Agree and feed back on the most important thing for each section.

Get Active 1 is what PSHE will be about: learning with each other and from each other. All of us learn and develop at school and in our wider lives outside school. We learn at school, in the playground, going shopping, at the movies – we may not realise it but we are learning all the time. This is part of what we call 'Personal Development'.

PERSONAL DEVELOPMENT = Life + The Universe + Everything

Source 1 Wherever we go, whoever we talk to, we are always learning.

Get Active 2

In pairs, look at the photos in Source 1. What personal development might be happening in each of the situations?

PSHE lessons are just one place where we can think about things that are important to each of us, and how we live in the world.

The letters PSHE stand for:

Personal
Social
Health
Education

Get Active 3

The word bank includes some of the topics you will be learning about in your PSHE course this year. Organise the words under the PSHE headings (Personal, Social and Health).

In your groups brainstorm some other topics you think might be covered under each of the headings.

Word Bank

Me and my family   Eating well   Saving pocket money
Feelings   Making choices   Donating to charity
Good communication   Not smoking   Exercise
Working with others   Friends

As well as learning about different topics, PSHE is also about doing things.

✓ learning with each other
✓ learning from each other
✓ bringing your own ideas and thoughts
✓ sharing them together
✓ listening to each other
✓ finding out what you have in common
✓ thinking about what is important to you

Get Active 4

Think back over the activities you have done in this lesson. Did they include using any of the skills in the checklist on the right?

Chapter 1 Starting out

2 How will we work together?

> **In this lesson you will learn:**
> ★ about the values of this PSHE course
> ★ how to create a Group Agreement for the class to work together in a safe and positive way.

We all have ideas by which we live, for example 'it is important to help other people', 'we should treat other people the same way we would like to be treated', and so on. Sometimes we call these ideas 'values'.

Your PSHE course will help you to develop a set of values – as shown in Source 1, the rainbow diagram.

Rainbow diagram with bands reading, from outer to inner:
- Know that each of us is unique
- Gain good information to make choices
- Develop decision-making skills
- Understand our emotions and feelings
- Enjoy what we learn
- Feel safe and supported to say what we think
- Listen to and consider what other people say

Source 1 PSHE Values

Get Active 1

In pairs, look at the rainbow of PSHE values in Source 1 and identify one example of something the class could do to make sure everyone works within these values.

The values in Source 1 are one way of describing how you can work with each other in PSHE. Another is to use these to develop a Group Agreement. A Group Agreement outlines the rights and responsibilities you share.

In PSHE each of us has the right to …
Be heard.

So each person also has the responsibility to …
Listen to others when they speak.

In PSHE each of us has the right to …

So each person also has the responsibility to …

In PSHE each of us has the right to …

So each person also has the responsibility to …

Source 2 An example of a Group Agreement

Get Active 2

Work together in small groups to come up with a Group Agreement. It should outline the rights and responsibilities you think you should share in PSHE. Use the example in Source 2 to help you.

All groups should feed back their ideas to everyone to help come up with a Group Agreement for your class.

Get Active 3

Can you think of examples of Group Agreements in everyday life? For example, the Highway Code is a Group Agreement which has become a law. A more informal example is the acceptance of speaking quietly and only when necessary in a library, allowing others to concentrate.

Children and young people in Scotland were asked to come up with a Charter setting out how they would like to be treated. The Charter in Source 3 is what they came up with.

Get Active 4

If you were given the opportunity to ask adults in this country to listen to you, what would you include in your charter?

A Charter for Young People

Get to know us

Speak with us

Listen to us

Take us seriously

Involve us

Respect our privacy

Be responsible to us

Think about our lives as a whole

Think carefully about how you use information about us

Put us in touch with the right people

Use your power to help

Make things happen when they should

Help us be safe

Source 3 *Protecting Children and Young People: The Charter (Scottish Government)*

Lesson 2 How will we work together?

3 Where are we going?

> **In this lesson you will learn:**
> ★ how to identify your individual characteristics
> ★ how to present yourself confidently to others.

Get Active 1

Look at the information about Amir Khan in Source 1 and give one example from his life of a strength, an achievement and a possible area for development. Use the definitions below to help you.

Strength: a strong point or good characteristic

Achievement: a success or accomplishment

Development: growth or progress towards a goal

Amir Khan (born 8 December 1986) is a British boxer from Bolton, Lancashire. He went to Devonshire Road Primary School, Smithhills High School and Bolton Community College in Bolton. He was a hyperactive child and 'a born fighter', according to his father, who encouraged him to take up boxing. His hero is Muhammad Ali.

Khan is a Raja of the Janjua Rajput clan of Pakistan, which has a long and well-documented history of warrior kings and a strong martial reputation.

In 2004 he won a silver medal at the Olympic Games in Athens. Amir celebrated his 21st birthday on 8 December 2007 by retaining his Commonwealth lightweight title against Graham Earl in Bolton.

Amir Khan fights child cruelty – he is the NSPCC's latest ambassador for children. Amir has supported the NSPCC since 2004. As NSPCC ambassador, he works to help children understand what abuse is, encourages them to talk about abuse, and ensures they know where to turn to if they need help.

Source 1

Get Active 2

Now think of yourself. What are your strengths, achievements, and areas in which you could develop?

You may not think you have achieved anything remarkable. Achievements are not only world record events; there are small and simple things we do that make a difference to other people. Can you think of something you have done that made you or someone else proud or happy?

Read Source 2, the interview with Jamie Oliver, the well-known chef, and see how he got started.

Was it always your ambition to be a chef? If not, what did you want to be when you were older?

Yeah, I think when I was younger I always knew I wanted to be a chef. I wasn't really positive until I had left school, and it was the only thing that I was good at. I went and worked in France, but they were so good and I was really rubbish at cooking, so I just put my head down, and the more I worked the more fulfilling it was.

Can you remember when you first cooked a proper meal? What was it and how old were you?

My first meal was a full monty roast dinner for my family, and we had roast chicken with all the trimmings, and I had done stuffing. I was probably around eleven.

What tips can you give me to impress as a chef?

I think keep things simple, but just do them really, really well … Stick to what you know, do it really well, because when people try and do really complicated things they get flustered and things start to burn!

Source 2

Get Active 3

Think about your hopes for the future. For each hope or goal, what would be the simple steps to start you on that journey? For example, if you hope to be a pop star or famous musician – do you know how to read music? Sing in tune? Play a musical instrument? Do you need to start by learning to do one of those things?

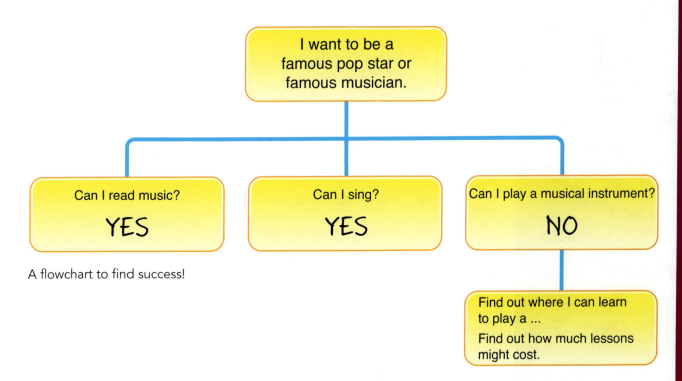

A flowchart to find success!

Lesson 3 Where are we going?

2 Healthy routines

4 What do we need to do to keep healthy?

In this lesson you will learn:
★ what 'being healthy' can mean
★ the importance of healthy routines in life.

Starter activity

What does 'being healthy' mean? If you were going to find out if someone was a healthy person, what kind of questions would you ask them?

Get Active 1

Design a questionnaire that helps you to find out if First Years in your school lead a healthy lifestyle. Start by working with another person to come up with five questions that would help you to decide. Don't just think about exercise and 'junk' food; what else affects a person's health? Are these your five best criteria for what we mean by healthy living?

Ten Ways to Stop Spreading Infections

✓ 1. Wash hands before touching food
✓ 2. Use a handkerchief/tissue when coughing or sneezing
✓ 3. Make sure used tissues go in the waste bin
✓ 4. Don't share combs and hairbrushes
✓ 5. Cover cuts with a dressing/plaster
✓ 6. Have vaccinations
✓ 7. Shower or bath regularly
✓ 8. Don't pick scabs or spots
✓ 9. Wash hands after going to the lavatory
✓ 10. Never spit

Source 1

Get Active 2

If we build healthy routines into our lives we can help to keep ourselves and others healthy. Look at the list in Source 1 of what you can do to stop infections spreading. Work with a partner to come up with an example of an infection or disease that might be prevented if you took each action suggested.

Get Active 3

Is your school a 'healthy school'? Imagine you are giving out awards for this. Work in groups to think about how you would rate these areas in your school, and give reasons for why you choose these ratings. As judges you are looking at the areas in Source 2:

	Excellent	Good	Not bad	Poor	Awful
Food					
Playgrounds					
Getting around the school					
Lessons					
Behaviour					
Help and support					
Pupils' views					

Source 2

Get Active 4

Go round the class completing this sentence: 'Healthy people are those who …'

Chapter 2 Healthy routines

5 What is my personal health profile?

In this lesson you will learn:
★ that an appropriate balance between work, leisure and exercise can promote health
★ to assess your own health profile.

Starter activity

Think back over the last 24 hours. Name one healthy thing you ate or drank, and one healthy activity you did. In a small group tell each other what you chose, and find out if others think you are healthy too.

Source 1 Being healthy means …

- Eating healthily.
- Balancing leisure, physical activity and rest.
- Making sensible decisions about alcohol, cigarettes and other drugs.
- Valuing and respecting yourself and others.
- Caring for the environment.
- Building good relationships with family and friends.
- Keeping safe.
- Dealing with stress or worry.
- Enjoying growing up.

Get Active 1

Look at the drawing and read the labels in Source 1. Think back to your questionnaires about health from the last lesson. Is anything missing from the picture?

1. First, it's time to reward yourself for what you are already doing well. Choose three areas from the picture where you are already doing something healthy, for example 'I make sure I get eight hours sleep every night'.
2. Now choose three areas where you think you need to make improvements to your lifestyle to become healthier. For example: do you eat five portions of fruit and vegetables each day? If not, set that as a personal learning goal.

Get Active 2

What about exercise? In the speech bubbles are three typical excuses that a person might use to explain away why they don't take more exercise.

Come up with a quick one-sentence response to each that might get them to think again.

> None of my friends does it.

> I'd rather be on the computer, watching TV or chatting with friends.

> It's not cool.

Get Active 3

How important are teeth to good health?

Imagine there's a 'Smile of the Year' award! Your task is to make a training schedule for a person who wants to win the award, by sending a daily text message reminding them what to do for the whole of the next week.

Cum up wiv 7 gr8 txt msgs that wld help them win ;-)

Get Active 4

Write out your personal action plan for healthier living.

6 What decisions can I make about healthy eating?

> In this lesson you will learn:
> ★ how to make decisions about foods that affect your health
> ★ information to help you make healthier choices about eating.

Starter activity

Your life involves making choices. Think back over the day so far, from the time you woke up until now. What choices have you made today that could affect your health? These could be choices about washing, food, exercise and so on.

Get Active 1

Look at Source 1, the balanced plate of the Five Main Food Groups, and make a meal plan for your family for a week.

The eatwell plate

Use the eatwell plate to help you get the balance right. It shows how much of what you eat should come from each food group.

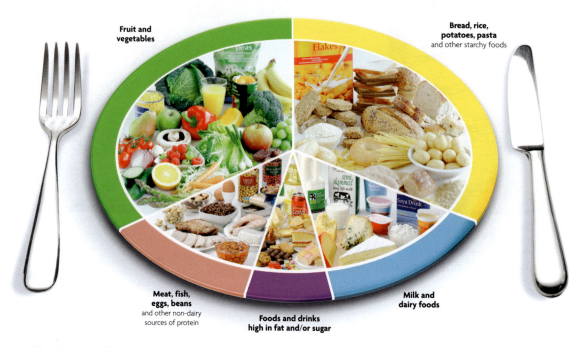

Source 1 The Eatwell Plate

Chapter 2 Healthy routines

14

The food traffic light system

If we want to eat a healthy diet, one of the key things we should be doing is trying to cut down on fat (especially saturated fat), salt and added sugars.

With traffic light colours, you can see at a glance if the food you're looking at has high, medium or low amounts of fat, saturated fat, sugars and salt in 100g of the food.

Red = High   Amber = Medium   Green = Low

So, if you see a red light on the front of the pack, you know the food is high in something we should be trying to cut down on. It's fine to have the food occasionally, or as a treat, but try to keep an eye on how often you choose these foods, or try eating them in smaller amounts.

If you see amber, you know the food isn't high or low in the nutrient, so this is an OK choice most of the time, but you might want to go for green for that nutrient some of the time.

Green means the food is low in that nutrient. The more green lights, the healthier the choice.

The food traffic light system

Get Active 2
Now look at the system of traffic light colours displayed on foods, and suggest how you'd plan the family shopping, based on your meal plans from Get Active 1.

Get Active 3
Finally, let's look at additives in foods. Read the information in Source 2, and decide which you'd avoid if shopping for food for children.

An example of a traffic light label on food

If you look on food labels you will often see an 'E' with a number next to it. Most of the processed food we eat would not exist without these additives. You can tell what kind of additive it is by looking at the 'E'-number.	
E100 to E180	Colouring to make colourless food look more appetising
E200 to E297	Preservatives that artificially make food stay fresh by slowing down the growth of bacteria
E322 to E495	Emulsifiers and stabilisers keep different parts of a food together, for example air and liquid in ice cream
E620 to E640	Flavourings; some are natural, but artificial ones have E-numbers: they add flavour to food
E950 to E967	Sweeteners are used instead of sugar for artificial sweetness

Source 2

Get Active 4
What is the one thing you would remove from the world that would instantly make it a healthier place? Why?

3 Substance misuse

7 What do we mean by 'drugs'?

In this lesson you will learn:
★ to explain what a drug is
★ some of the risks involved with taking legal drugs.

Starter activity
What does the word 'drug' mean? Discuss this question and come up with a class definition.

An international definition of the word 'drug' is:

'A substance people take to change the way people feel, think or behave.'

This is the definition of a drug given by the United Nations Office on Drugs and Crime. Is this similar to your class definition? If not, how does it differ? Which definition do you think is better? You now have a definition of the word 'drug', but what else do you know about drugs?

Get Active 1

To make sure we all have some basic information about drugs, answer the following questions in groups, and then feed back your answers to the rest of the class:

1 What forms could a drug come in?
2 In what ways do people take drugs?
3 What effects do drugs have? How might they change the way a person feels, or thinks or behaves?
4 What substances that are legal to use are also drugs? Could medicines be included in this definition?
5 Are tobacco and alcohol also drugs? What is it about them that fits the United Nations' definition above?
6 Do gases, glues and solvents fit the United Nations' definition above? What is it about them that make them a drug?

Legal but dangerous?

In the chart in Source 1 you will find factual information about three drugs. None of these three drugs is illegal, but all of them can be associated with major health problems.

Get Active 2

Look at the chart in Source 1 and the images on this page and choose one key fact about each of the three types of drug (alcohol, tobacco and volatile substances) to feed back to the rest of the class. Your key fact should be what you think is most important to know about the effect of the drug.

It is important not to chase or scare someone who has been using volatile substances, as a change to heart rate can kill. Can you think of other dangers from using volatile substances?

It may be against the law to drink alcohol in some public places. Do you know if your town or area has rules about this?

Get Active 3

Think back over the lesson. Work in pairs to complete this sentence: 'If I was invited back to talk to Primary 7s at primary school, the one really important thing I have learnt about drugs that I would tell them is …'

Smoking in public places was banned in Scotland from 26 March 2006. What do you think were some of the reasons for introducing the ban?

	Alcohol	Tobacco	Volatile substances
What else might it be called …	Booze, drink, bevy	Fags, ciggies, smokes	Glue, aerosols, lighter refills
How would I take it …	As a drink to swallow	Smoked in manufactured cigarettes or hand-rolled, in pipes and cigars	Inhaled (breathed in) through the nose or mouth
If I took it I might feel …	Talkative, happy, friendly or angry, argumentative, dizzy	Able to concentrate more, or relaxed – or dizzy, sick	Silly, dizzy, drunk, argumentative and aggressive
If I use it I might risk …	Being sick (vomiting), having an accident, getting into fights, damaging my liver, doing things I wouldn't normally do	Very lined or wrinkled skin, heart disease, lung infections, cancer	Sickness, blackouts, changed breathing and heart rate, coma

Source 1

Lesson 7 What do we mean by 'drugs'?

Chapter 3 Substance misuse

8 Fact or fiction?

> **In this lesson you will learn:**
> ★ what influences your perception of drug use and how this can differ from reality
> ★ some key facts about young people's drug use in the UK.

In Lesson 7 you learnt what the word 'drug' means. However, many people may not think of drugs in the same way, and how they think about drugs may be shaped by the media.

Starter activity

Look at the headlines in Source 1 and use them to discuss the following questions:

- Where do people get their ideas and information about drugs?
- What impressions do these headlines give you about drugs?
- Do you think information about drugs from newspapers, magazines, television or the Internet is accurate? Give reasons.

Criminal offences by children at 600 a day

Half of all suspects have been using cannabis

Alarming rise in child drug dealers

One in five pupils tried drugs

Source 1

Get Active 1

The media can negatively affect ideas about drug use by what they choose to report and the language they use. For example, look at this headline:

'First Year pupils in our schools regularly drink alcohol!' This could be changed to say: 'In a group of 100 pupils in First Year, 97 do not drink alcohol regularly.'

Both statements are true but they present very different pictures of young people and alcohol use.

1. What message does each of the statements above give about First Year pupils drinking alcohol? Discuss how the messages differ.
2. Look again at the headlines in Source 1. Rewrite each one to give the opposite message – by changing negative statements to positive ones.

As we have seen, headlines and reports in the media like those in Source 1 can negatively or positively affect what people think about drugs. Have your thoughts about young people and drug taking been affected by what you have seen, read and heard? Try the quiz below to find out.

Get Active 2

Look at the questions below and decide which you think is the correct answer for each one.

Young People and Drugs – Fact or Fiction?

1. In a group of 100 pupils aged 13 how many do not smoke regularly (once a week)?
   a) 96 b) 69 c) 76

2. In a group of 100 pupils aged 13 how many had not drunk alcohol in the last week?
   a) 45 b) 79 c) 89

3. In a group of 100 pupils aged 11 how many had not taken illegal drugs in the last month?
   a) 77 b) 97 c) 55

4. In a group of 100 pupils aged 13 how many had not smoked cannabis during the last year?
   a) 19 b) 49 c) 98

Statistics obtained from:
Scottish Schools Adolescent Lifestyle and Substance Use Survey (SALSUS) National Report 2008

Get Active 3

In pairs, discuss the following question:

Why do we overestimate the numbers of people who we think are:

- smoking cigarettes
- drinking alcohol
- using illegal drugs?

Not all the media is negative. D-world is a good website to find realistic information about health and young people:
http://www.drugscope-dworld.org.uk/wip/24/index.htm

9 How do we reduce the risks?

In this lesson you will learn:
★ to identify how risk relates to you
★ to explain some risks associated with drug use
★ that choices can be made to reduce some risks.

Starter activity

In pairs, put the pictures and captions in Source 1 in order of risk. Which is the most risky and which is the least risky? Be ready to feed back why you have chosen this order.

Not using a pedestrian crossing

Riding a bike without a helmet

Stroking a dog you don't know

Source 1 How risky?

In the Starter Activity you may have come up with different orders and reasons why one situation is riskier than another. So what is risk?

Risk is ... the chance that harm might be caused.

When we think about risk we need to think about two things:

1 The *what* – the harms that might happen to us.
2 The *might* – the likelihood that harm will happen to us.

From the definition of the word 'risk' given above, and the work you have done on the effects of drugs in Lesson 7, it is clear that there are risks in taking legal drugs. You will explore some of these risks in the next activity.

Most parents who smoke don't want their children to start smoking.

Get Active 1

Work in pairs to discuss the situations below. For each one:
1. Identify the harm that might happen.
2. Assess the likelihood that harm will happen.

You can use the thought bubbles on this page to help you with ideas as well as coming up with your own.

- Smoking one cigarette a day on the way to school.
- Secretly helping yourself to alcoholic drinks from home.
- Using one of your friend's prescription pills for a headache.
- Playing truant from school.
- Drinking alcohol while alone with your boyfriend/girlfriend.

> You can quickly become dependent on the nicotine in tobacco, and then it is very hard to give up smoking.

In each situation in Get Active 1 you identified different risks associated with taking legal drugs.

As well as thinking about what risks there are in certain situations, it is also important to think about how the risk can be reduced. In the next activity you will need to think about how you can reduce the risk of harm from tobacco, alcohol and other legal drugs.

> Alcohol slows down the brain and body, making it more likely you could have an accident.

Get Active 2

1. For each situation in Get Active 1, discuss as a whole class how the risks of harm could be reduced. For example, not smoking in the first place will mean that you don't risk becoming dependent on nicotine.
2. Now in pairs make a list of ways that could prevent someone from starting to use tobacco, alcohol and other drugs. For example, one way would be having a strong friendship where you have agreed to support each other not to smoke. Try to come up with five ideas.

> Many pupils who truant from school get bored and find themselves using drugs – legal and illegal.

> Alcohol changes behaviour. For some people this leads to aggression and fighting.

Get Active 3

This lesson has contained a lot of information and encouraged you to think about a lot of ideas. Use this sentence stem to focus on one key thing you have learnt:

'If I get into a risky situation I could now …'

> Giving your own prescription medicines to someone else to use is against the law.

> About eight young people in Scotland die every year from sniffing volatile substances.

Chapter 3 Substance misuse

10 How do drugs affect people?

In this lesson you will:
* think about the different ways we view people who use drugs
* learn how drugs affect physical, mental and emotional health
* learn that there is help and support available for people who have problems with drugs
* consider how to help someone who wants to stop smoking.

Starter activity

'Drugs' – what do you think of when you hear that word? Brainstorm ideas with the rest of the class.

Drugs are all around us. We read about them in newspapers and magazines, see them on television and hear about them on the news and maybe even from friends. Often, we hear about them in relation to addiction or to drug addicts. When you hear somebody described as a drug addict, what do you think of?

Get Active 1

1. Work together in groups to describe a 'drug addict'. Think about what they look like, where they live, how they spend their time, who their friends are and so on.
2. Feedback and discuss your ideas with the rest of the class.

Now that you've thought about the ways in which drugs can affect people, let's look at some of the effects of drugs that are commonly used in the UK. Two of those drugs – alcohol and tobacco – can be used legally.

Source 1

22

Get Active 2

1 Work in pairs to draw a person who is dependent on a drug.
2 Label your drawing to explain the different effects this drug can have. Source 1 opposite should give you some ideas.
3 Is anybody else affected by your person's drug use? If so, include this in your labelling, explaining how and why they are affected.

Tobacco and alcohol are the most commonly used drugs in the UK and a lot of people are dependent on them. Most of those people don't enjoy feeling dependent – feeling you must have another cigarette or drink to get through the day can make life difficult. That's why a lot of people try to stop. It isn't easy for people who are dependent to stop smoking or drinking alcohol on their own. They need help and support.

I was smoking around a packet a day and had been smoking for about fifteen years when I decided to give up. I wanted to give up because I hated being dependent on cigarettes and it was becoming socially much more unacceptable to smoke. It was difficult to give up as I craved cigarettes all the time for around two months. At the start I avoided being around other smokers so there was no temptation! It got much easier and, two years on, I love being smoke-free!

I always wanted to give up smoking before I was 30, and this year my doctor told me I should give up for health reasons, so I decided I had to stop. I signed up to the NHS Stop Smoking Service, who sent me encouraging emails and helpful leaflets. The smoking ban meant I could sit inside smoke-free pubs with my friends – I didn't miss having to go outside in the wind and rain with the other smokers! Now I've been an ex-smoker for three months, I've saved lots of money and I've got a lot more energy.

Source 2

Get Active 3

Look at Source 2 and read what the people say about giving up smoking. Imagine you know someone who is trying to give up. In groups, list three things you could suggest to encourage them.

Get Active 4

Give one reason to explain why talking about 'drug dependency' is more helpful than talking about 'drug addiction'.

4.11 What do we mean by 'family'?

In this lesson you will learn:
- ★ about different types of families
- ★ that our relationships affect our wellbeing.

Source 1 Different types of family

Starter activity

Look at the photos in Source 1 and see if you can come up with some answers to these questions:
- What do you think these families might have in common with each other?
- Does a family always live together? Why might they live in different houses or places?
- What makes a group of people a 'family'?
- Family members don't always get on with each other. What sort of things can go wrong on a day-to-day basis? For example a brother and sister falling out over whose turn it is to wash up the dishes.

Get Active 1

Family arguments are easily started, but not so easy to stop. Read Source 2 and then discuss these questions:
1. How do you think Harry and Tom felt when they heard their parents arguing?
2. How far was Tom to blame for this argument starting?
3. How far was Harry to blame for this argument starting?
4. What could each family member do to calm the situation?
5. What could each family member do to avoid repeating it?

Relationships, sexual health and parenthood

David and Sheila have been married for fourteen years. They have two children, Tom aged twelve and Harry who is nine. David's job has got more difficult recently, and he is staying longer in the office. Sheila has returned to work, to bring extra money into the home. Both parents can find themselves tired and irritable when they get home from work.

One summer evening Tom couldn't be bothered to do the washing up, even though it was his turn. Instead, he went out on his bike with some mates. Harry hadn't done his homework and was moaning about it. Sheila and David got into an argument about who had given Tom permission to go out, and why Harry hadn't finished his homework.

David started having a go at Sheila for being too tired after the day at work to discipline the children. A really loud shouting match started between them. Harry and Tom overheard Sheila saying, 'It's not just down to me to get the boys to behave. You're their father. It's as if you're married to the office …'

Source 2

Get Active 2

No family is perfect and there are all sorts of things that family members can do to get on. Read the speech bubbles to see what other young people have said.

In small groups, write up a list of top tips for young people and adults who are living together as a family. Come up with at least five positive things that young people could do or say. Now find five things that adults could do or say. Think about why these are good examples and explain how they could help families to live in harmony. Here is an example:

Young People	Adults
1. I will walk the dog when it's my turn on the rota.	1. If you do what you agreed on the rota then I won't nag!

Get Active 3

Imagine your family has been voted 'Family of the Year' by the whole country. You have been chosen to go on stage and accept the award. Your acceptance speech must end with this sentence: 'In my family I would most like to thank … because …'

Share your sentence with at least one other person in the class. Then when you get home, if you feel like it, share it there too!

Get Active 4

Some people who have known each other for a really long time sometimes say they feel 'part of the family'. Sometimes joining a club, an activity or religious group can also give us a 'family' to which we can belong. Who would you bring together in your ideal family household?

Don't be cheeky!

Try and get on – make compromises. That way you get somewhere.

Just be honest with your parents, because if you lie to them … well they know, and it doesn't really help.

My mum has a lot to cope with – the twins and me and my brother. But I do what I can to help, like washing up and stuff.

Just try not to fight with your brothers and sisters because that puts a strain on everything, especially your parents.

12 Is commitment important in relationships?

In this lesson you will:
- ★ think about marriage and stable relationships
- ★ discuss marriage and other partnership ceremonies
- ★ look at the significance of commitment vows.

Starter activity

The government says it is important for people your age to learn about marriage and stable relationships. Why do you think this was included in the list of topics that schools should cover?

People may feel they are happiest when their lives are stable, when they know they can depend and rely on the people around them. Many people choose to live their lives as part of a couple.

Get Active 1

Think about people you see on television or read about in books who live together in couples. Give some examples and for each, answer the following questions:

1. Why do you think they have chosen to be together?
2. What do you think makes them happier being together than being alone?

When two people live together, as discussed in Get Active 1, we talk about them having made a 'commitment' to each other. Some people choose to show their commitment to and love for another person by taking part in a ceremony. Marriage and civil partnership ceremonies are two examples of these, as shown in the photos on these two pages.

Some people choose commitment ceremonies to celebrate their marriage (a man and a woman) or civil partnership (same gender couples)

Get Active 2

Look at the photos on these two pages and the vows below. Use them to list the things that people do in marriage and civil partnership ceremonies to demonstrate their love and commitment to each other.

Vows are special promises that people make at important times in their lives. At a marriage or civil partnership ceremony, the two people repeat vows to each other.

For example, in a Christian religious ceremony the bride and bridegroom face each other. One at a time they take each other's hands and say:

I, … take you, … ,
to be my husband/wife,
to have and to hold
from this day forward;
for better, for worse,
for richer, for poorer,
in sickness and in health,
to love and to cherish,
till death us do part,
according to God's holy law.
In the presence of God I make this vow.

Signing the register makes the marriage/partnership legal

Kissing at the wedding ceremony celebrates the couple's happiness

Get Active 3

Above are the traditional vows people use in a Christian marriage ceremony, but people often write their own vows. Work in pairs to write your own version of a set of marriage or civil partnership vows. Decide what you think is important for two people to promise to each other.

Many people celebrate their wedding as part of a religious ceremony – this is from a Hindu wedding

Get Active 4

Just because two people are in a committed relationship doesn't stop things going wrong. Look again at these words:

'for better, for worse,
for richer, for poorer,
in sickness and in health'

Why should couples think about the ups and downs of being in a relationship before they have their ceremony?

Exchanging rings and keeping promises to each other form part of most weddings – this is a Jewish 'ketubah' – a marriage contract

Get Active 5

Go back to one of the couples you thought about in Get Active 1. If you could give them one piece of good advice about marriage or partnership, what would it be?

13 How can we contribute to family life?

In this lesson you will:
★ think about the roles and responsibilities of parents, carers and children in families
★ consider how relationship skills can be built
★ practise the social skill of appreciation within relationships.

Starter activity

Living together as a family involves everyone doing their share. Think of one thing that is your particular responsibility in your home, or a task that you always do. Explain what it is to your partner and whether you like doing it, or not!

Not everyone will like all the tasks that need to be done around the house. Should different members of a family have specific roles in the household? Look at how one family (who have one son and one daughter) share the various household responsibilities.

Task	Example family
Cleaning the kitchen	Dad helped by daughter sometimes
Cleaning the bathroom	Mum
Cooking	Dad
Doing the ironing	Dad – sometimes other family members help out
Tidying the living area(s)	Son and daughter
Tidying bedroom(s)	Each does their own
Looking after pets	Daughter
Domestic shopping (food and cleaning products)	Mum
Jobs outside the house: gardening, car washing	Dad and son

Get Active 1

1. Work as a group and either complete the chart that your teacher will give you or draw up your own with the tasks in the chart on page 28 listed in one column and a column for each group member to complete for their family.
2. Now think about how the tasks in your family were agreed in the first place and discuss the following questions in your group:
   - Did you choose your tasks, or were you told which tasks you had to do?
   - Do you think the distribution of tasks in your family is fair?
   - If you don't do your task, does another family member always end up doing it for you?

It's not just sharing out the tasks that can cause problems in a family. There can be all sorts of reasons for family rows and upsets. Here's a list of some of the things that families find help their communal life to run more smoothly.

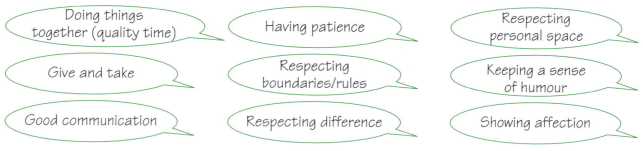

- Doing things together (quality time)
- Having patience
- Respecting personal space
- Give and take
- Respecting boundaries/rules
- Keeping a sense of humour
- Good communication
- Respecting difference
- Showing affection

Get Active 2

1. Work together as a group and discuss the speech bubbles above. Construct a 'diamond 9' by ranking each item in a diamond like the one on the right. The item that you think is most important should go at the top and the one you think is the least important should be at the bottom. Make sure you discuss why you have ranked them in that order.
2. There are nine items in the speech bubbles. If you had to add a tenth one, what would it be?

The statements in the 'diamond 9' all describe positive ways of getting along with each other, but when living communally, we can sometimes take each other for granted. We might forget to thank a family member who helps us or whose company we really enjoy. Think about the people you live with. Is there someone who you would like to thank?

Get Active 3

1. Why might it sometimes be important to make the time to say 'thank you' to the people who are around you everyday?
2. Make an appreciation card or poem that you could give to someone whose contribution to your life you value. Look at the cards on the right to give you ideas.

Get Active 4

Apart from the tasks you undertake, what do you think your family members would say is the main contribution you make to family life?

14 What's happening to me?

In this lesson you will learn:
★ that everyone experiences physical changes as they grow up
★ about ways to manage these changes.

Starter activity

Look at the pictures of the boy and girl in Source 1: they have begun the journey through puberty. What changes might they have experienced? Use the following three headings to help you think about this:

- Physical – How have their bodies changed?
- Emotional – How have their feelings changed? (Happier? More stressed?)
- Social – How have their relationships with family and friends changed?

Source 1 Puberty means 'grown-up' or 'adult'. A person going through puberty is experiencing the changes that take them on a journey from being a child to becoming an adult.

When it comes to the word 'puberty', lots of people think it is all about sex. When it comes to words like 'sex' lots of people get embarrassed. People might use slang, 'dirty words' or family names to describe parts of their bodies. These words might upset some people, and one way to make sure that no one gets upset and that we all understand each other is to agree which words to use. Here is a list of words that describe genitals – sexual parts of our bodies.

Male

Penis   The fleshy organ through which urine and semen leave the body.

Testicles   Round 'balls' in which sperm are produced.

Scrotum   The bag of skin containing the testicles.

Female

Vulva   The name of the whole area of the genitals.

Vagina   An opening passage through which a baby is born.

Clitoris   A small bump about the size of a pea. It gives sexual feelings.

Get Active 1

Look at the worksheet which your teacher will give to you, listing how male and female bodies change during puberty. Sort these changes by ticking the right columns: whether they happen to

- girls only
- boys only
- both girls and boys.

Get Active 2

One of the important things we must remember to do as our bodies change at puberty is to pay more attention to keeping clean.

Imagine you are going to take part in a television reality show. You will live in a house that has no washing machine or tumble dryer and only limited supplies of hot water. You are only allowed to purchase five hygiene products, for use between all of you (male and female combined – sanitary towels/tampons are automatically provided for girls and do not count in your total number of products). What should you take and why?

You will need to think about these things: germs, skin, hair, sweat, teeth, feet, clothes.

Right now you are aged between eleven and twelve, just like everyone else in your class – apart from your teacher, who's probably about 150! If you look around you at people your age you will notice that some are tall, and others are shorter. Some people have big feet and others have small feet. The fact is that puberty happens at different rates and not at exactly the same time for each person. It is natural to worry about the fact that you feel different – that you aren't like everyone else seems to be, but at some point everyone will catch up and reach their own adult size.

Get Active 3

Think about the things that are good about you – just as you are now. Perhaps you have a nice smile, or are good at sports, or maybe you're a great friend to be with? Each person has special things about them.

Work together in a group. Each person should write down the names of everyone in the group including themselves. Next to each name write something that you like about that person. It might be something about their personality, the way they look, or something else. Remember, you must write something about yourself too.

Get Active 4

Think back over all the things you've talked about in this lesson. You will have heard information about puberty and names for the genitals. Some of the feelings and emotions that have been discussed included how we feel about all maturing at different rates. You may still have questions that you would like answered. On a slip of paper write down one question that you would like to ask privately, fold it up and place it in the 'Ask it Basket'. You do not have to write your name next to the question.

15 Why do I feel like this?

> **In this lesson you will learn:**
> ★ how feelings change as we grow and mature
> ★ ways to build confidence to be able to cope with these changes.

Starter activity

Can you remember how you felt on the very first day at this school? Were you nervous, excited, worried? Did it seem huge? Were you worried about getting lost? Did you know anybody else coming to this school? Was the journey different? Did you travel on your own? Compared with then, how have your feelings changed? Why might you feel more relaxed about your school now?

What is 'puberty'? This is the term that describes the changes that take you on a journey from being a child to becoming an adult. These changes include things that happen to our bodies as well as our emotions and our relationships with other people. The hormones that make all the physical changes happen also affect our feelings. We just can't see them!

People are at different places on the journey – some are happy not being too grown-up and others can't wait to be adults. Some are even-tempered whilst others find their moods change quickly, finding one minute they're feeling really happy to go along with friends and the next they don't want to talk to anyone!

problem page

Dear Problem Page,

I am 11 years old. I started secondary school in August, and I am really unhappy.

My Mum and Dad split up during the summer holidays. My Mum has moved house with me and my sister — we moved from our old town and now we're in this new place.

Most people made friends in primary school and they seem to have lots of friends here at secondary school. I don't know anyone and it's not been easy to make friends. I don't want to bother my Mum with this as she's finding it hard enough anyway.

What advice can you give me?

Yours sincerely,

Jenny

Dear Problem Page,

On Friday and Saturday nights my friends get to stay out later because they don't have school the next day. My Mum and Dad won't let me go anywhere, and if I invite friends home I get really embarrassed by them – so I don't ask anyone round. How can I get my parents to treat me like a grown-up?

Yours sincerely,
Hardeep

Dear Problem Page,

I'm 13 and I've got really bad acne. It feels like everyone's looking at me and I hate it so much that I just want to hide away. I'm sure my friends think I'm the ugliest person in our group. Loads of my friends boast about being able to get a snog - I can't. No one would fancy me.

Yours sincerely,
Brian

Get Active 1

Look at the letters from young people of about your age. They all feel that they're facing problems that are part of changing and growing up. Work with a friend to write replies to some of these letters. Imagine that you are an Agony Aunt or Uncle; your job is to give advice, reassurance and sources of help.

Get Active 2

Imagine that in your local area secondary schools are contributing to a teenagers' magazine. Your school has been asked to focus on the topic of 'puberty and growing up'. One way of helping people who feel worried or distressed is to give them confidence to explore activities which they will enjoy. Think of ideas for articles that would encourage pupils to explore new interests and things to do. You might also want to think of people who could be interviewed – especially local people who already work in ways that help and support young people. You and your team need to produce plans for the sort of articles the magazine would feature for First Year pupils.

Get Active 3

Look at the field of words in Source 1. This describes some of the emotions that young people feel as they go through all the changes of puberty. Not everyone finds it easy to talk about these emotions. Imagine you could tell advisers on a young people's helpline how to prepare to talk to young people. Which two of these emotions might come up most often in young people's conversations? Why did you choose those two emotions?

Source 1 Field of words

embarrassed worried sad bothered different
stupid bored amazed interested just OK
fantastic nervous annoyed scared curious angry

Lesson 15 Why do I feel like this?

5 Assessing risk

16 How do we manage risky situations?

In this lesson you will learn:
★ how to respond in risky situations
★ some ways to keep yourself safe.

Starter activity
Think back to Chapter 3, and remind yourself of the meaning of the word 'risk'.

Here's one way of defining 'risk':

'the chance of something bad happening'.

Risk is the chance that harm might be caused. When we think about risk we need to think about two things:

- The *what* – the harms that might happen to us.
- The *might* – the likelihood that harm will happen to us.

Take the example of an aeroplane crashing. The chance of being harmed if the crash does happen is high. However the likelihood of this happening is low, because so few planes crash compared to the large numbers that fly every day.

Can you think of any other examples that show the difference between the 'what' and the 'might'?

Get Active 1

Where do you think you are most at risk? Here are four locations where accidents might happen to someone your age. In which do you think an accident is most likely to happen? Rank them in order of most dangerous location to the least dangerous:

1. On the road or in car parks.
2. In or around the home.
3. In school.
4. Whilst doing sport.

You may be surprised at the answers to this. It isn't always obvious when we might be at risk – so we need to think and plan to keep safe. This will help us reduce the risk of something bad happening. Risk can never be completely ruled out or our world made completely safe, but there are ways in which we can think about a situation and reduce the risks.

How to deal with a risky situation

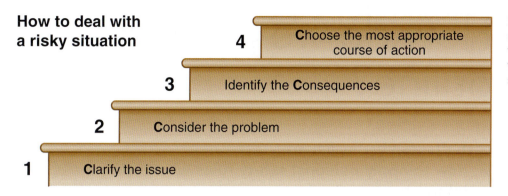

Source 1 There are four steps you could take to help you work out what to do in different situations.

Get Active 2

Look at the situations on this page, and use the four steps in Source 1 to work out what you could do.

It's a sunny day in the summer holidays and you and your friends are spending the day in the park at the end of your street. Some of the group decide that climbing to the top of one of the trees would be a great idea.

You and your friends are at a party. Everyone is helping themselves to food and drink. People are behaving as if they are a bit drunk. You want to keep in with everyone in your group, but you don't want to drink alcohol. One of your mates offers you a bottle of something alcoholic.

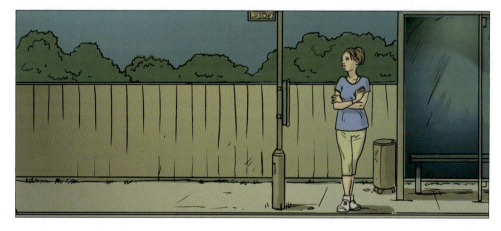

You have spent the day at a friend's house. You have been told you have to be back home by 6p.m. You thought you had allowed plenty of time but you've missed the bus and have run out of minutes on your mobile phone. It's getting dark. You know you're going to be in trouble if you're late.

Get Active 3

Think about how you would complete this sentence:

'The most important safety message I've learned from today's lesson is … because …' Share your sentence with one other person.

17 How do we keep safe online?

In this lesson you will learn:
★ how to apply personal safety rules when using the Internet.

Starter activity

In small groups, list three functions that people use the Internet for. Share these with the rest of the class.

There are commonsense rules for everyday life, and there are commonsense rules for using the Internet. For example, when buying online there are sensible precautions that you should take – only shopping on a reliable website, making sure that you only give credit card information on a 'secure' site and so on.

In Lesson 16 you started thinking about ways to keep yourself safe. Personal safety is important on the Internet too. Look back at your list of functions that people use the Internet for. Are there instances where people would need to think about their personal safety?

Get Active 1

A very popular use of the Internet is chatting to people online. Work with one other person to come up with three personal safety rules when using the Internet to chat online. Remember to agree between you why you think they are necessary.

Get Active 2

Julie is a friend of Sammi – they are both twelve. Sammi has moved away from the area and her father has bought her a computer and a mobile telephone to help her keep in touch with her friends. Sammi has had several contacts in a chatroom by email and text from a person she does not know. She is not sure how to deal with this and keeps sending Julie email messages asking for advice.

With the person you worked with on Get Active 1, work out your response to Sammi's questions in blue text on the emails.

MESSAGE 1

Hi Julie! I'm feeling really down. I have not made any new friends and I wish we could move back to Stonehaven. I've been online and have been getting messages from a guy called Mark. He seems really nice. He's told me he's 17 and used to go to our old school – isn't that a coincidence? I've never chatted to a guy in a chatroom before. What should I ask him?

MESSAGE 2

Hi Julie, I got a message from Mark last night. He asked if he could meet me and we could spend the day in Stonehaven. I said my Dad would not let me do that, but Mark said I should not bother letting Dad know. I am tempted to go and meet him, but I don't know what to tell my Dad about where I'm going. What do you think?

MESSAGE 3

Hi Julie! I'm feeling much happier. My Dad's bought me my own mobile phone and Mark says I should give him the number so he can text me. He says it will be easier and he can reach me any time, even in school! I thought that I would give him my number to keep him quiet. Do you think that's OK? What would you do?

MESSAGE 4

Hi Julie! I know you said that I shouldn't have given Mark my mobile number but he kept on at me, so I did last night, in the chatroom we both use. Anyway, I wish I hadn't because it's been a real hassle at school. Mark kept sending me text messages on my phone – he was a real nuisance. I think one of the teachers noticed and was suspicious. Should I tell my teacher? I wish I hadn't given Mark my mobile number. Has this kind of thing ever happened to you?

MESSAGE 5

Hi Julie! I sent a message to Mark asking him not to keep sending me text messages and he replied straight away and says that we should meet and he can come and pick me up at school tomorrow. I don't think I told him what school I went to but I can't remember what I told him now. I am terrified in case he turns up. What should I do?

Get Active 3

Discuss together as a class what you would advise if a friend came to you with this problem. Your teacher will reveal to you what happened in Message 6. Do you think this is a good solution to the problem?

Get Active 4

Young people sometimes know more about the Internet and modern technology than their parents. What advice about Internet safety would you give to your parents or to someone new to it?

18 How can we tackle bullying?

In this lesson you will learn:
★ how to prevent bullying from happening
★ the importance of speaking out against bullying.

Everyone – children, teachers, adults – can help put a stop to bullying.

There are lots of reasons why some people start bullying, and why others are bullied. There is something about all of us that others might pick on, but bullying, at school or outside school, is always wrong, no matter what.

Starter activity

There is never a justifiable reason for bullying. Ever. Bullying at school can happen for lots of reasons. Why do bullies single people out? What sort of things do they pick on? In groups, see how many examples you can think of.

Source 1

Peter's story

We had this PE teacher and he thought anyone who wasn't good at games was stupid. I'm really small for my age and not much good at PE. He started picking on me in lessons. Then he started calling me a wimp and other things. It doesn't sound much. I mean, he never touched me or pushed me around or anything, so when I tried to tell my Mum, it did sound rather pathetic.

Rachel's story

It all started when my Mum got married again. I liked my new stepsister. She was older than me and I really looked up to her. When she moved in, though, her friends came round all the time and made life difficult for me. She kept on putting me down with comments about how I looked. She said if I told Mum I'd be in trouble and I'd split the family up. Then she started threatening me and saying that if I didn't tidy up her room she'd tell Mum that I was rude to her. I did try talking to Mum but she was so happy I didn't want to spoil things for her.

Source 2

Anne's story

I was new at the school – joining halfway through the year – and break times were the worst. This group of pupils used to hang around by these seats that were out of sight of the school windows, and that's why they went there. At first they were friendly and chatty, and being new I was really pleased that they let me be part of their group. Then they wanted me to buy cigarettes for them. I said I didn't smoke and that's when it started. They got all the other pupils in the class to completely blank me.

Source 3

Get Active 1

Read the stories about young people's experiences of being bullied in Sources 1, 2 and 3. Work together in pairs to come up with three ways in which each young person could begin to tackle their situation.

Get Active 2

How do you think your school creates a positive atmosphere where pupils support and help each other? Are there additional things that you can suggest? In and around school, what could pupils in First Year do to prevent bullying happening in the first place?

Get Active 3

Bystanders are people who do not act while someone else is being bullied. Sometimes they may join in with name calling, even though they are not the ringleader. Have you ever seen bullying happening and not known what to do? In Source 4 are some statements made by young people who were bystanders. What would you say to each one to encourage them to help?

Get Active 4

Read the words in Source 5 that other people have written about bullying. They all focus on the hurt and pain that bullying can cause.

Compose a verse or piece of prose, in no more than five lines, that could inspire somebody to speak out against bullying or gain the courage to do something positive.

Source 5

> 'Sticks and stones may break my bones but words will never hurt me.'
>
> (Often quoted but not at all true.)

> 'Why are they all so big, other children? So noisy?... Lived all their lives in playgrounds. Spent years inventing games that don't let me in.'
>
> Roger McGough

> 'Give us another 10p or get another bash For being you.'
>
> Mick Gowar
>
> © Mick Gowar

Speech bubbles (Source 4):
- I knew it was wrong to do nothing, but I was worried the bullies would come after me too.
- He showed me the text message he'd got. It was really mean.
- My friend went on and on about being bullied – I got tired of listening to her.
- I stood in the circle and listened while the others called her names ...
- There weren't any adults around when it was happening.

Source 4

"First Day at School" by Roger McGough from *In the Classroom* (© Roger McGough 1976) is printed by permission of United Agents (www.unitedagents.co.uk) on behalf of Roger McGough.

19 How do I work best with others?

Meeting and working with others

In this lesson you will learn:
★ that people have multiple roles and responsibilities in society
★ to think about how different roles help make a group successful
★ why positive relationships are helpful when working in groups.

This is Ajit. Ajit is a ...

Son
Annoying brother
Pupil in First Year
Good friend
Good footballer
UK Citizen
Scout
Stamp collector
Grandson
Hindu

Source 1

Starter activity

Each of us has many roles in life. Look at the picture of Ajit and the number of different roles he takes in Source 1. There are probably many more that aren't even listed. Think of yourself: what roles do you have in your life?

Get Active 1

'Tallest Tower'

This competition is to see which group can build the tallest tower from newspaper and sticky tape. The rules are simple:

1. Each group will have exactly the same number and size of sheets of newspaper.
2. Each group will have a roll of sticky tape.
3. You are not allowed to fix your tower to any surface in the room - it must be freestanding.
4. Each group is only allowed ten minutes to do it!

Get Active 2

Sometimes working in a group or team isn't a happy experience. Things go wrong or the group never seems to gel. Working in pairs, list all the reasons you can think of that get in the way of a team being happy and successful.

Think about actions, words and attitudes.

Choose three things from your list and write each one on a separate piece of paper. Your next task will be to see if you can solve some of the problems that come up in unhappy teams.

Get Active 3

Imagine you are a team of five people taking part in a television game show. When you practised at home you did really well. Now that you're in the studio things are going wrong and a couple of members of your team seem to be determined to wreck your chances by messing about. It's time for a break in filming. What can you say or do to get all the team working together again?

You are not allowed to argue, fight or bribe them and you can't tell them to go home. How could you persuade them to 'get on board' again?

Get Active 4

What do you think is the best thing you can contribute to a team?

20 What do I want and how do I get it?

In this lesson you will learn:
- ★ to think about the positive things you want in the future
- ★ to create steps to help you achieve your goals
- ★ how to turn steps into targets.

Starter activity

Is it easier to work towards a goal that you have set for yourself, or one that has been set for you by someone else?

Get Active 1

Sheryl lives in a happy neighbourhood and knows other people in her street, joins in local activities and helps her Mum serve tea at the local senior citizens' Friendship Club.

Sheryl wants to go on her school's First Year trip to France, because she enjoyed the school trip when she was at primary school. Her parents have said that the primary school trip was less than a year ago and she has had a family holiday since then. They only feel able to contribute 50 per cent of the cost of this trip. They tell her that if she can raise the other 50 per cent she can go.

Sheryl

- What steps can Sheryl take to raise the rest of the money?
- What can she do on her own?
- Will she need to work with other people?
- In what way might she need other support from adults?

Get Active 2

In the Starter Activity you began to look at the reasons for setting your own personal goals. This activity gives you the chance to practise setting goals by working out steps to help someone solve a problem.

- On her way to school Tracy regularly sees Archie, and she would like to become friends with him. They have never had a real conversation with each other but they recognise and smile at each other and nod 'hello'. *Tracy's goal: To become friends with Archie.*
- Daniel's younger brother and sister really irritate him, and he tends to lose his temper when they are around. He knows that he has said hurtful things to them and would really like to be able to control his temper. *Daniel's goal: To control his temper when he's around his brother and sister.*

- Hari is having real difficulties in one of her school subjects. She wants to improve her chances to do better. Her teacher is willing to help but points out she is not following her homework schedule and has fallen behind. Hari has several pieces of overdue homework in more than one subject, and doesn't know where to start. *Hari's goal: To improve her study skills.*

Discuss solutions for these people, using the Goal Setting Planner your teacher will give you.

In Get Active 2 you helped other people by breaking down their goals into achievable steps and finding solutions to the possible blocks that got in their way.

We sometimes call these steps 'targets'. You may have already been setting targets at school, or perhaps this idea is new to you.

The targets you set have to be achievable, not just a hope or a wish. The best way of setting a target is to think of them as 'SMART' targets:

S Specific, for example, I will improve the presentation of my work by always putting the date and underlining titles. Not – I will make my work look better.

M Measurable, for example, I will improve my punctuality to 100 per cent this term. Not – I will try to be on time.

A Attainable, for example, I will attend choir club every week. Not – I will sing the solo in the next school concert.

R Realistic, for example, I will learn 10 new words in Spanish each week. Not – I will learn 50 new words in Spanish each day.

T Time Specific, for example, I will aim to achieve these targets by the next half term holiday. Not – I will do this as soon as I can.

Get Active 3

Here are some goals written by pupils your age. Turn them into SMART targets. Which bit of SMART will you use to help you in each case?
- I'll get completely up to date with my homework.
- I'll try to visit my auntie more often.
- I must improve my piano playing.
- I am going to keep my bedroom tidy all the time.
- I'll get round to my revision before the exams start.

Get Active 4

How could you apply the SMART target idea to something you want to achieve in your own life?

21 What do I do if I need help?

> **In this lesson you will learn:**
> ★ to think about sources of help and support
> ★ to research local and national services
> ★ to identify key messages to use when help is needed.

Starter activity

What are the 'emergency services' (name at least three) and what single method can we use to contact all of them?

Get Active 1

Most local areas have all sorts of services available to help people in their community. Which ones do you know? Here are a few to get you started:

- Citizens Advice Bureau
- Civic centre/town hall
- Doctor/GP
- Health clinics
- Library
- Young people's walk-in or drop-in centre

Can you think of any more?

Do you need to be a particular age to use any of the services listed above or the ones that you have thought of?

How easy is it to find out the locations and opening times of the different services?

Get Active 2

Sometimes unexpected situations occur and we have to make quick decisions. We may not always get it right, but often one course of action will be better than another. Look at the scenarios in Sources 1, 2 and 3 and decide which answer you think is best in each case.

Source 1

Some friends are the only people on the beach near home when one of them sees a person out in the water waving frantically.

What are the pros and cons of each of the following possible actions:

- **a** Give a friendly wave back.
- **b** The strongest swimmer in the group goes to see if anything is wrong.
- **c** Use a mobile or other phone to dial 999.

A group of friends have been to a party. On the way home one of them collapses. The others think this person might have been drinking alcohol – and they are underage.

What are the pros and cons of each of the following possible actions:

a) Leave the collapsed person where they are, get home on time and on arrival tell an adult.

b) Wait with the collapsed person while one of the group phones for an ambulance.

c) Wait with the collapsed person while others go back to the party for help.

The next-door neighbour is on holiday and a window is open at the back of the house.

What are the pros and cons of each of the following possible actions:

a) Go into the neighbour's back garden to investigate.

b) Dial 999 to ask for help.

c) Tell an adult from another nearby house.

Source 2

Source 3

Get Active 3

As you get older you get more freedom to be out and about, on your own or with friends. This means accepting some responsibility.

Use the Internet to research how best to react in emergency situations. Here are two websites that may help you:

www.hedgehogs.gov.uk.
This site has tips and quizzes on travel safety.

http://www.juniorcitizen.org.uk/kids/index.php
This site has tips and quizzes about safety with dogs, electricity, fire, food, railways and vandalism, and many more topics.

Research some key safety messages for your allocated topic area. Focus in particular on how to react in an emergency situation. Come up with three key things that you think pupils in your class will find useful to know.

Get Active 4

This chapter cannot cover all the different situations in which an emergency might arise. Consider one way you could use your local library as a source of further helpful information.

7 Managing personal money

22 What could we do with money?

In this lesson you will learn:
★ about possible uses of money
★ about managing money through budgets
★ how our money can help support others.

Starter activity

Some people say about money, 'Easy come, easy go'. Is that really true? As a First Year pupil you are not yet old enough to have a paid job, so where does your money come from, and when you've got it what do you use it for?

Get Active 1

In the Starter Activity you thought about where money comes from and how it might be used, but you probably didn't think about how you actually manage it when you've got it. In three groups, imagine you have been given £25 to spend on setting up one of the charity events in Sources 1, 2 and 3 at your school. There is a shopping list of items for each event and you will need to budget carefully to buy as much as possible from the list.

Senior Citizens' Tea Party

Decorations
Cups/saucers/plates (25)
Tea/milk/sugar
Raffle prize
Book of raffle tickets
Fairy cakes (25)
Bridge rolls (25)
Biscuits
Paper napkins
Small take-away gift (25)

Source 1

Sponsored Walk

Printed sponsorship forms
Chequered flag for finish
Armbands for marshals (25)
Clipboards for stewards (10)
Pens/biros (10)
First aid kits (2)
Plastic cups
Water
Prize for person who raises the most sponsorship
Participation certificates
Maps of the route

School Play

Printed programmes
DVD, CD or cassette of music
Printed tickets
Interval refreshments
Advertising posters
Special green face and body make-up
'Fright' wigs (2)
Fangs/vampire teeth (2 sets)
Stage blood
Spray-on cobwebs

Source 2

Source 3

Get Active 2

In Get Active 1 you practised budgeting in groups to support a school charity event. Individuals also support charities and have to decide how much of their personal income they might want to give.

Read Ami's weekly budget in Source 4. Ami has £3 left to spend. She wants to give some to charity. Work with someone else to come up with some advice for Ami:

- How much should she give to charity each week?
- Which charity should she choose?

Get Active 3

In this lesson you have learned about income, expenditure and the value of budgeting. How can you put this learning into practice in your own life?

Ami's weekly budget
Income   £5   for carrying out tasks in the home
Expenditure   £1   into savings account – earning 5% interest
              £1   into a piggy-bank (for birthday gifts)
Balance   £3

Source 4

Lesson 22 What could we do with money?

23 Do I spend or do I save money?

In this lesson you will learn:
★ to explore options and choices about what you do with your money
★ to think about the value you place on different types of purchases.

Starter activity

Imagine that you're about sixteen to seventeen years old and you have just finished your SQA exams. If you could go anywhere in the world, where would it be and what would you do there? If you were given millions of pounds, what would you do with so much money?

Get Active 1

People have very different attitudes to what they do with their money.

In Source 1 are three types of people. In pairs, brainstorm the advantages and disadvantages of being each kind of person.

Source 1

A spend, spend, spend person

A save, save, save person

Chapter 7 Managing personal money

48

A spend some, save some person

Get Active 2

Imagine that you take a balanced approach to money and want to save some of it. Where do you think the best place is to save your money, and why?

1. In a piggy bank.
2. In an ordinary account (often called a 'current account').
3. In a savings account.
4. In a stocks and shares portfolio.

After one year, without you taking any money out, what do you think would have happened to your investment?

	Stays the same	More money	Less money
Piggy bank			
Ordinary account			
Savings account			
Stocks and shares portfolio			

Get Active 3

In Get Active 2 you were thinking about a balanced approach involving savings. How can we balance our approach when it comes to spending? One way is to think about our priorities.

In Source 2 are nine things that you might spend your money on. In pairs, rank them in order of priority. Remember that you will have a limited amount to spend, so you will have to make some choices.

Get Active 4

Complete the following sentence: 'A new piece of information I've learnt about money is …'

> Birthday present for Mum or Dad
> Burger meal with group of friends
> Donation in a charity collection box
> Entertainment activity with friends (e.g. cinema or bowling)
> Latest fashion item of clothing – just like your friends have
> Lend money to a friend who needs it
> New CD by favourite singer/group
> Sweets/ice cream/crisps
> Top up your mobile phone

Source 2

Lesson 23 Do I spend or do I save money?

24 How will I earn money in the future?

In this lesson you will learn:
★ about the meaning of the word 'career'
★ what careers might suit you in the future
★ how you might begin to plan a career.

Starter activity

Most people want to achieve things in life, but get distracted from their goals. You can stay focused by coming up with your own personal motto. For example, somebody who is good at putting things off could use the motto 'Do it now!' What personal motto would help keep you focused on your goals?

Actor
Newsreader
Newsagent
Nurse
Paperboy/papergirl
Parent
Pop star
Postman/postwoman
Professional footballer
Shop assistant
Soldier
Supermarket checkout assistant
Teacher
Traffic warden
Vet
Window cleaner

Source 1

Get Active 1

Is there a difference between 'having a job' and 'having a career'? Look at the list in Source 1, and decide whether you think each person is doing a job or having a career.

Get Active 2

Pupils in First Year told us that when they hear the question 'What do you want to do when you grow up?' they want to say things like:

'Give it a rest, I'm only eleven!'
'I don't know.'
'Be an astronaut.'
'Not a lot.'
'Be famous.'
'I haven't really thought about it.'

Of course, you might have thought about it … but then again maybe you haven't. No one should feel under pressure to make such a big decision at this stage in life. You will change a lot as you grow up, and new sorts of jobs and careers could be available in the future.

However, thinking about your personal strengths and interests can help you start the journey. Make a spider diagram like the one in Source 2, with you at the centre and all the things you're good at and your interests around you. Spend some quiet time seeing where your diagram takes you.

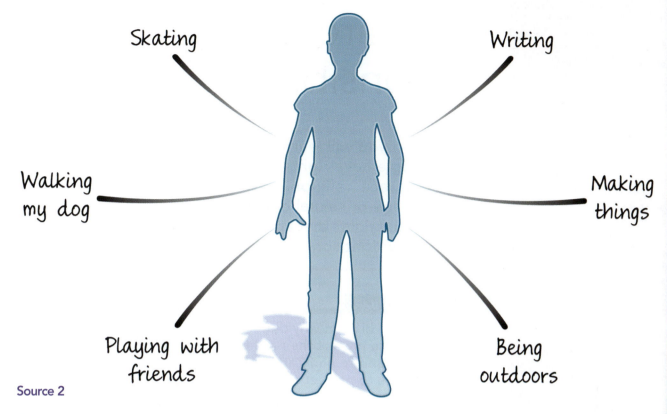

Source 2

Get Active 3

Even the most glamorous of careers will have a tedious side to it. There will always be routines that need to be followed and qualifications that need to be gained. Let's think about the example of 'soldier' from Get Active 1. The recruitment adverts usually show them on active duty (hiding in forests, climbing mountains, jumping out of planes – all looking very exciting!), but Source 3 lists some of the practical things a soldier needs to learn to do.

What would be the practical tasks and routines for each of the following:

- member of a boy/girl band.
- running a pub
- fitness instructor at a leisure centre
- dancer in a musical
- cosmetic surgeon
- on-board crew for an airline
- nanny in a celebrity family
- morning TV presenter.

Get Active 4

Complete this sentence: 'When I leave school, a statement I would like to read about myself in my school record is:...'

1. Be awake, up and ready to work at a specific time.
2. Follow set routines for preparing your uniform.
3. Tidy your living area.
4. Clean your equipment.
5. Practice drill and exercise routines.
6. Develop teamwork skills.
7. Take responsibility for specific tasks.

Source 3

What are my rights and responsibilities?

In this lesson you will learn:
★ that people have rights regardless of their different race, religion, culture, ability or disability, gender, age or sexual orientation
★ some of the rights that apply to you as a young person
★ that every right comes with its own responsibility.

Starter activity
Think back over history: why did human beings need to write rules and laws to protect their rights? (Clue: think about freedom, protecting life and so on.) Can you think of any examples of laws that were made to protect children?

Get Active 1

Since you've been born, there have been many changes to laws in Scotland: for instance from 1 October 2007 shopkeepers were not allowed to sell cigarettes to people under eighteen years of age. Why do you think this was done? How does this help to protect young people?

There are also laws and rules to make sure that you and others are not discriminated against. For example only a short time ago all decisions in some schools were made by adults alone – there were no School Pupil Councils or other ways that pupils could voice their opinions. Now government departments in charge of education expect schools to keep young people involved and to find out what they think.

When and where are there chances for you to be involved in rule making?

Get Active 2

Take a look at three rights that young people have in Source 1. They come from the United Nations Convention on the Rights of the Child and are called 'Articles'. The United Kingdom has signed up to this Convention so they are your rights too.

Work in pairs to discuss one of these Articles. Come up with answers for these questions:

- Do you think you and your friends get a real chance to exercise this right?
- What might get in the way, or stop you fully benefiting from this right?
- What do you think would have to change to make this right apply 100 per cent in your life?

Article 12 – Children have the right to say what they think should happen, when adults are making decisions that affect them, and to have their opinions taken into account.

Article 15 – Children have the right to meet together and to join groups and organisations, as long as this does not stop other people from enjoying their rights.

Article 17 – Children have the right to reliable information from the mass media. Television, radio, and newspapers should provide information that children can understand, and should not promote materials that could harm children.

Source 1

If children have a **right** to be protected from conflict, cruelty, exploitation and neglect, then they also have a **responsibility** not to bully or harm each other.

If children have a **right** to a clean environment, then they also have a **responsibility** to do what they can to look after their environment.

If children have a **right** to be educated, then they have the **obligation** to learn as much as their capabilities allow and, where possible, share their knowledge and experience with others.

Source 2

You might want to research more information on the Convention of the Rights of the Child – there are 42 Articles! The website which will help you find out more is:
http://www.unicef.org.uk/tz/resources/assets/pdf/rights_leaflet.pdf

Rights are extremely important. Without them we might have no education, be sent out to work for very low wages, work long hours, have no freedom to choose what we could watch on TV or access on the Internet.

So it's important to protect rights. One way of protecting rights is to remember that every right comes with a responsibility. Each person needs to get involved in protecting their rights and be responsible for other people's rights.

Source 2 shows how the United Nations Convention on the Rights of the Child explains how a right can carry responsibilities.

Get Active 3

If you were a member of your School Pupil Council, how would you ensure that the responsibilities in Source 2 were taken on by the pupils in your school?

Get Active 4

This chapter is about changing. It asks you to think about growing up and gaining a better understanding of how the world around us operates and how we can influence things in it. Complete this sentence: 'As I get older I think an important right in my life will be …'

Chapter 8 Changing

26 What makes each of us an individual?

In this lesson you will learn:
★ about people different from ourselves
★ to appreciate some of the differences between people
★ to think about showing respect for other people's feelings.

Starter activity

Think of a word to describe you that begins with the same letter as your first name, for example 'I am Jolly Jane'.

Get Active 1

Look at the photos in Source 1, which represent the cultural variety of people in Britain today.

- Are any people in the images familiar to you in some way?
- Do you recognise national or religious clothing? Symbols, for example?
- What differences do you notice?
- What do all these people have in common?

Source 1

Get Active 2

Work with another member of your group to draw a picture of each other. Don't worry about being a great artist, as you can add labels to describe what you have drawn. You can draw any part from head and shoulders to the whole body – that is up to you!

You will need to chat to each other as you do your drawings so that you can find out individual things about your partner. For example you can label 'Shoe size 3', 'Height 130 cm', 'Hair colour brown', 'Eyes blue', and so on.

Write the name of the person you have drawn above the picture. Ask them how they want their name to appear.

Get Active 3

Now your task is to interview each other using the 'Who are you?' interview form your teacher will give you. This will cover a variety of likes and dislikes such as favourite TV programmes, favourite food, pet or no pet, favourite pop group and so on.

Include special things about the person that make them unique. What positive things can you find about your partner that makes them unique?

Get Active 4

You will probably have learnt a lot about your partner in the class today. Now think about some things you learnt about yourself during this exercise; what made you feel you are unique?

27 How can I make and keep good relationships?

In this lesson you will learn:
★ that relationships affect everything we do
★ that positive relationships are important in our lives
★ that relationships can cause strong feelings and emotions.

Starter activity

A United States President once said: 'If we must disagree, let's disagree without being disagreeable.' What do you think he meant?

Get Active 1

You may already have your own 'blog', or perhaps you have a personal page on a website. If you have one you will probably have remembered all the safety rules we looked at in Lesson 17, How do we keep safe online?

Today is your opportunity to create an 'I'd be a great friend to have …' page on your imaginary online site. Use the example below to create your personal page. Think carefully about the drawings and phrases you will use to get your message across. Think about your personal characteristics. What are your interests and hobbies? What qualities have you got that make you a great friend? Try to identify five different things.

FRIEND AVAILABLE

My name is Frankie, aged 12, and I'm the friendliest, funniest, funkiest mate you could ever hope to have! I like dogs (NOT cats!) and rollerblading, and I'd love to meet other people to share my free time with. Text me on the number below. No bores should bother to reply!

Get Active 2

Even the best of friends find that they sometimes disagree or even fall out with each other. Do you think having arguments together is a natural part of being friends? What sorts of things do friends argue about? Come up with a list of things that might cause an argument between friends.

Get Active 3

Read the examples of situations where friends fall out or disagree. Work together with someone to come up with simple suggestions for solving each problem. What would you have to do and what would your friend have to do to keep the friendship going?

- You were invited to spend the night at a friend's house. Half an hour before you were due to leave, your friend telephones to cancel. The next day you find out that someone else was invited instead of you.
- You and your friend have decided to join an after-school club. There are two activities you both want to take part in, but they are both scheduled for the same time.
- For the last couple of months you have been going round to your best friend's house every day after school. You enjoy it but are beginning to feel you'd like to do other things too.
- You and your friend have done something wrong, and now your parents have found out. You tell the truth but your friend lies and doesn't admit to being involved.
- You've lent a favourite item of clothing to a friend and s/he returns it dirty and with a hole in it.

Get Active 4

Look at the graffiti sheets that have been started for you and decide on one thing you would put under each heading.

The Number One friendship skill is ...
Being a good listener

The best thing I can offer another friend is ...
My loyalty

A best friend would never ...
Bad mouth me

We all need friends in life because ...
It's good to have someone to play with

Preparation task for Lesson 28: Collect from home three items that represent important aspects of your life. These might include a piece of sports equipment, a picture or photograph, a sentimental toy, a hobby magazine and so on. Put them in a bag to bring to the next lesson.

9.28 Who am I?

Personal identity and self-esteem

In this lesson you will learn:
★ that your identity is affected by a range of factors, including a positive sense of self
★ how to feel accepted and 'normal' as a member of your class
★ that self-esteem can change depending on personal circumstances.

Starter activity

'All I'd really like out of life is to be normal.'
What do you think the young person who said this meant?

Get Active 1

At the end of Lesson 27 you were asked to bring a 'Bits of Me' bag to this lesson, so you should have with you a bag containing three items that represent important aspects of your life. You now have one minute to share information about what those items represent for you. When everyone in your group has listened to each other, make a quick note of how you felt having everyone listen to you for a full minute.

Get Active 2

Read the stems in Source 1 and complete the sentences.

> 🙂 It's easy to share how I feel when …
> 😐 It's hard to share how I feel when …
> 🙂 I feel best when …
> ☹️ I feel uncomfortable with people when …
> 😐 I'm most comfortable with boys and girls when …
> ☹️ At school I'm most concerned when …
> 🙂 I'm at my happiest when …

Source 1

Get Active 3

'Great things are achieved not by impulse, but by a series of small things brought together.'

Vincent Van Gogh 1853–90, artist of *'Sunflowers'* and *'Starry Night'*

We all have different abilities, talents and ambitions, and yet we are often encouraged to be modest and not 'show off' about what we do well.

But today is different: you now have the chance to talk with one other person about yourself. You must mention what you are talented at, what your best skills are, what personal qualities you have that make you special, and what things you have accomplished, or perhaps even achieved awards for. There is an example that somebody else gave in Source 2.

'I am talented at illustrating my work with neat drawings. I'm skilled at map reading and never get lost if I've had time to plan a route. One of the personal qualities that makes me special is that I'm friendly and other people feel comfortable talking with me. I have an amazing imagination that takes me to the places I dream about.'

Source 2

Get Active 4

Think about how you would complete this sentence:

'The most important positive thing I've learned about myself from today's lesson is … because …'

Share your sentence with one other person.

Lesson 28 Who am I?

29 What am I good at?

> **In this lesson you will learn:**
> ★ to think about your own personal qualities
> ★ to reflect on your personal strengths
> ★ to appreciate how other people see you.

Starter activity

'You can't judge a book by its cover.' What do you think this means?
If you could choose your own personal qualities, for example being friendly, cheerful, adventurous, sensitive, what would you choose? Take a few minutes to think about this and come up with three qualities that you would like to have.

Get Active 1

Now that you've had the chance to think about the qualities you wish you had, here's an opportunity to hear about the positive qualities your classmates know you do have. Working in groups, select 'positive quality' squares for each other (or your teacher will hand out cards for you to give each other).

Give your reasons for selecting these qualities – and invent extra ones if you wish.

Positive Qualities

FUN	SENSIBLE	HAPPY	HARD-WORKING
TRIES HARD	LIKABLE	CONFIDENT	QUIET
FRIENDLY	CAREFUL	SOCIABLE	LOYAL
THOUGHTFUL	WARM-HEARTED	CONSIDERATE	TRUSTWORTHY
GENEROUS	KIND	HUMOROUS	RESPONSIBLE
HONEST	POPULAR	CHEERFUL	GOOD LISTENER
BRAVE	FAIR	INTELLIGENT	POLITE
BRIGHT	REASONABLE	HELPFUL	CAPABLE
GREAT SENSE OF HUMOUR	LAID BACK	TOLERANT	RELIABLE
AMIABLE	TENACIOUS	CALM	SUPPORTIVE

In this unit of work you have begun to recognise that you are unique. Even though you are all in the same year group, and all around the same age, you are all different. You have special characteristics, talents and abilities that make you who you are.

We all have 'off-days' when perhaps we don't feel happy, can't seem to do anything right, get into arguments, or maybe even break things by accident. Nobody knows why this happens, but it does, and it happens no matter how young or old we are. It's at times like these that we need to know that we are still worthwhile – knowing that our peers think we are OK really helps.

Get Active 2

Now you have the opportunity to think about what your classmates are good at – and tell them so. In groups of six, each write your name at the head of a page and pass the paper to the person on your left. Each person writes a skill particular to the person named, folds the paper and passes it on. Are you surprised by the skills that have been listed for you?

Get Active 3

By now you will have begun to realise that you are valued by other people. You and other members of the class have identified several of your positive attributes and you will have done the same for them. Feels good, doesn't it? But even with all this positive feedback nobody will actually know how it feels to be you.

On a plain sheet of paper make a picture of what it feels like to be you. You don't have to be brilliant at drawing – you can use lines, shapes and colours to express how you feel and a few words too if that helps. What you do is up to you!

Get Active 4

Take a while to think about how you want to finish this sentence:
'I believe I am unique, and people in this class have recognised that I am skilled at …'

On your picture from Get Active 3 write your completed sentence.

30 Where am I going?

In this lesson you will learn:
★ to define what a personal 'goal' is and identify the role of goal setting in leading a successful and productive life
★ to identify different ways in which people become successful
★ to view yourself as having the potential to be a winner in life.

'Whatever you can do, or dream you can do – begin it. Boldness has genius, power and magic in it.'

Johann Wolfgang von Goethe, 1749–1832, German writer

Starter activity

The way to make our dreams come true is to do something positive to create an environment where they will happen. What we need to do is have a goal.
We need to focus on what we want and then plan a way to get it. What do you think a goal is? Do you have one? Have you planned a way to achieve it?

Get Active 1

On a sheet of paper complete the answers to the questions below:

1 What is the most important goal in my life right now?
2 If I could choose one thing that I would most like to happen in my life, what would it be?
3 How can I help to make it happen?
4 If I could learn to do one thing, what would it be?
5 If I could change one thing about myself, what would it be?
6 What is one way that I can make the best of myself?

Get Active 2

You now have the opportunity to hear from some successful people and then interview them so that you can learn more about the things they have done in their lives that enable them to feel successful. Source 1 contains some questions that you may like to ask them.

Get Active 3

So far in this chapter you have looked at setting goals, in order to plan where you're going, and interviewed some people who have achieved success in their lives. Now you are going to carry on looking at success by examining the importance of having positive role models. If you could choose one person as a role model, who would it be and why? Answer the questions in Source 2.

Interview questions

1. Of all the things you've achieved in your life – what are you most proud of?
2. Have you regarded anyone as a role model for yourself? If so, who and why?
3. What do you think is your most important triumph?
4. Did you set yourself any goals? If so, what were they?
5. Do you think planning and setting goals has been important in your life?
6. Who helped you achieve your goal(s)?
7. Would you have done anything differently?

Source 1

1. What is the name of your role model?
2. What part has s/he played in the world? Are they from history or connected with your community (perhaps a family member) or do they have another place in the lives of other people?
3. What is it that you know (or have learned) about this person that makes them special?
4. What is it about this person that made them an attractive role model?
5. What impresses you about them?
6. Are you similar to them in any way – and if so, how?
7. In what ways are you different from them?
8. If you were asked to write down one thing this person should be remembered for, what would it be?

Source 2

Get Active 4

In this lesson, and the previous ones in this chapter, you have learned about the positive qualities that people can have, for example caring for others, being kind and so on. What have you learned today about people who earn our admiration? What makes them special and worth looking up to?

31 How can we communicate better?

In this lesson you will learn:
★ about good listening skills
★ to practise speaking and listening to others
★ to identify ways that good listening can help you and other people.

Starter activity

Choose a subject that you think you could talk about for 'Just a Minute'. It can be anything that interests you or you feel you know a lot about: for example a hobby, a famous person, a sport, your favourite subject and so on.

Get into pairs, and each of you talk for one minute on your chosen topic. Try not to repeat yourself, pause too much, or end up talking about something else.

Take turns and time the other person. How easy was it for you and them to talk for one minute?

Get Active 1

In the Starter Activity you were probably concentrating on being a good speaker – but how good a listener were you?

Without help from your partner:

1. Write down the three most important facts or ideas you thought you heard while they were speaking.
2. Write down the three most important facts or ideas that you think you spoke about.

Read them back to each other – do your lists agree? Were you a good listener to what they were saying?

Sometimes we need to practise listening as much as speaking. Work together in your pair to identify up to five things that make somebody a good listener. Then explain them to the rest of your class.

Listening Skills assessment levels

4 'Active Listening' – you are paying attention to what they say and how they say it: their feelings about the subject.

3 'Hearing the Content' – you are taking in basic facts, opinions and so on.

2 'Superficial Listening' – you are going through the motions of listening but aren't really paying attention.

1 'Ignoring' – you know the other person is talking but you are not responding to them.

Source 1

Get Active 2

Work with a different person in a pair and play the 'Just a Minute' activity again.

This time, when you are the listener, choose one of the Listening Skill levels 1 to 4 in Source 1 and play the role of someone listening at that level. See if your partner can guess which Listening Skill level you were demonstrating.

Get Active 3

Obviously it feels good when someone is really listening to us. In what situations is it important to be a good listener when talking with others?

Work in a small group to come up with examples where being a good listener is vital when you are communicating with the people in Source 2.

Source 2

Teachers

Family members

Shop assistants

One of the Emergency Services

Get Active 4

Complete this sentence: 'My top tip for being a really good listener is …'

32 What does 'assertiveness' mean?

> In this lesson you will learn:
> ★ about the meaning of 'being assertive'
> ★ the difference between being assertive and being aggressive
> ★ to practise assertiveness skills.

Starter activity

Think of as many different ways as you can to say the word 'Yes', so that each time it has a different meaning.
Try saying it to yourself in your head …
- as if you really, really mean it
- as if you're not sure if you mean it
- as if you don't mean it at all.

Try out the different ways of saying 'Yes' with a partner, but don't reveal which is which. Could they guess the different feelings or thoughts you were having as you said each one? How could they tell?

Are there any other ways of saying 'Yes' which may have other thoughts or feelings behind them? For example saying 'Yes' but with such a big sigh that the other person knows you think it's a real hassle and really means you don't want to do it.

Get Active 1

Our tone of voice, the expressions we use, the speed at which we speak – all of these affect how our words are heard. Sometimes we say words but the way we say them might reveal different feelings or thoughts.

In the same way as 'Yes', the way we say 'No' to something can reveal our true feelings. Here are some words that describe different ways of saying 'No':

| timidly | ferociously | calmly | gently |
| aggressively | assertively | sweetly | |

Let's take two of these words that people sometimes mistake for each other: 'aggressively' and 'assertively'. Here are some definitions that could be used to explain the difference:

Speaking aggressively: attacking/being hostile/being offensive

Speaking assertively: declaring/being confident/being sure

Working together in small groups, make notes to answer and report back on these questions:

- Are there other ways you could explain the difference between these two ways of speaking?
- What could be the result of an individual/group/nation speaking to another individual/group/nation aggressively?
- Why could being assertive be a better way of dealing with a problem than being aggressive?

Get Active 2

Speaking assertively isn't always easy – especially when people put pressure on us to agree with them when we might have a different point of view or we want to say 'no'.

Look at the list of tips for being assertive and speaking assertively in Source 1. What do you think of them? Would they help you to be assertive without becoming aggressive? Why?

> **How to be assertive – some tips:**
> - Be sure you know what you want.
> - Sit or stand up straight – your body language should be relaxed but not casual.
> - Use a serious expression – match your expression to the words you use – look like you mean it!
> - Look directly at the person you are talking to.
> - Use a clear, firm voice.
> - Say what you want or need.
> - Listen to the other person.
> - Repeat your message as often as you need to.
> - Suggest alternatives that are acceptable to you – this could show you still want to be friendly with the other person even if you can't at first agree.

Source 1

Get Active 3

Your teacher will give you a scenario card that describes a situation in which the most sensible course of action would be to refuse to go along with the suggestion.

Work together in a pair to role play the conversation. In the first scenario person A acts as the 'persuader' and B as the 'asserter'; then A and B can swap roles or try another scenario card. After you have role played the conversation both ways, give your partner feedback on the good things they did to demonstrate they could be assertive without being aggressive.

Get Active 4

Look back over the different scenarios described in Get Active 3 where someone might need to be assertive. Can you suggest another scenario where this might be helpful?

33 What are the biggest challenges for me?

> **In this lesson you will learn:**
> ★ to think about your personal successes this year
> ★ to identify some challenges for the future
> ★ to consider how good communication can us help face challenges
> ★ to learn about 'Refusal Skills'.

Starter activity

As you come towards the end of this year at school, think back and identify an important success for you.

- This could be work-related, for example you did well in a test or produced a good project.
- Or it could be related to skills, for example you succeeded in a sport or activity/hobby/club that you hadn't experienced before.
- Your success could also be personal, for example you made good friends in new situations where you didn't know anybody very well.

Share your success with a partner – and listen to them describe theirs.

Get Active 1

You have just thought back over the last year. Now think forward to next year: are there going to be any challenges for you to face? What do you think they will be?

Work together in a small group to come up with two challenges that pupils might face as they move from one school year to the next. Write each one on a slip of paper. Your challenges will now be swapped with those of other groups – and your group's next task is to discuss what pupils can do to help them face the challenges on the slips of paper that you have been given.

Make a note of how pupils could face these challenges, ready to give feedback on any useful points for a class discussion.

Get Active 2

In the last activity you discussed how pupils can face a variety of challenges or new situations as they move up to the next year. Sometimes the advice might have been very specific, but often the advice could be turned into good general guidance: for example 'When facing a difficult problem it is always better to ask for help rather than worrying about it on your own.'

Work together in a group to come up with a list called:

'Good Communication – Five Ways to Face New Challenges'.

You will be asked to share your five ways with the whole group, so word them simply and clearly. Ensure that the pieces of advice involve good communication with others. The example above fits this category: it is about communicating with others to get support and help.

Get Active 3

Look back over this lesson and the two earlier ones about 'Confident Communication'. In them you have identified at least two useful ways of improving communication skills:

- Active Listening Skills
- Assertiveness Skills.

These will all help you become a better communicator.

However, as much as we want to be positive communicators, sometimes the skill we need when we feel we might be harmed or in danger is the skill to say 'No'. We call these 'Refusal Skills'.

Source 1 lists some simple techniques for saying 'No'. Practise these skills by moving around your group: each time you meet a different person say 'No' in a new way. Remember, it's not about the volume you use or an aggressive tone; saying 'No' in a calm, quiet way is often much more effective than raising your voice.

How to say 'No'

- Simply say 'No' or 'No thanks'.
- Be direct, for example 'No, I don't want to do that'.
- Be a broken record – repeat 'No' over and over again or use variations to make your point: 'No, I'm not interested' … 'Not me!' … 'No, never'.
- Walk away – if they won't accept your 'no' then it's time to go!

Source 1

Get Active 4

Think what rating you'd give yourself for how well you can use these different communication skills:

	I can do this really well	I'm fairly good at this	I need to practise this more
Active Listening			
Being Assertive			
Saying 'No'			

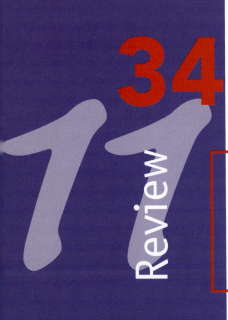

Hey, how are *you* doing?

In this lesson you will learn:
★ to review what you have learned in PSHE
★ to think about what you have accomplished on the course
★ to recognise your own skills, qualities and achievements.

Starter activity

You have covered many topics in this year's course. Here are some of the things you have learnt about:

- Being Healthy
- Staying Safe
- Relationships
- Substance Misuse
- Communicating Confidently
- Personal Learning Planning

Think back over the list and write down one or two key things you have enjoyed learning about.

Getting it Right for Every Child (GIRFEC) is the name of a big project across Scotland which involves everyone who works with children. It is based on research, evidence and best practice and is designed to ensure all parents, carers and professionals work effectively together to give children and young people the best start to improve their life opportunities.

Scottish Government ministers have set out a high-level vision for children and young people in Scotland:

> 'We have ambition for all our young people and we want them to have ambition for themselves and to be confident individuals, effective contributors, successful learners and responsible citizens. All Scotland's children and young people need to be nurtured, safe, active, healthy, engaged in learning, achieving, included, respected and responsible if we are to achieve our ambition for them.'
>
> *Getting it Right for Every Child 2008*

The diagram below shows this shared vision:

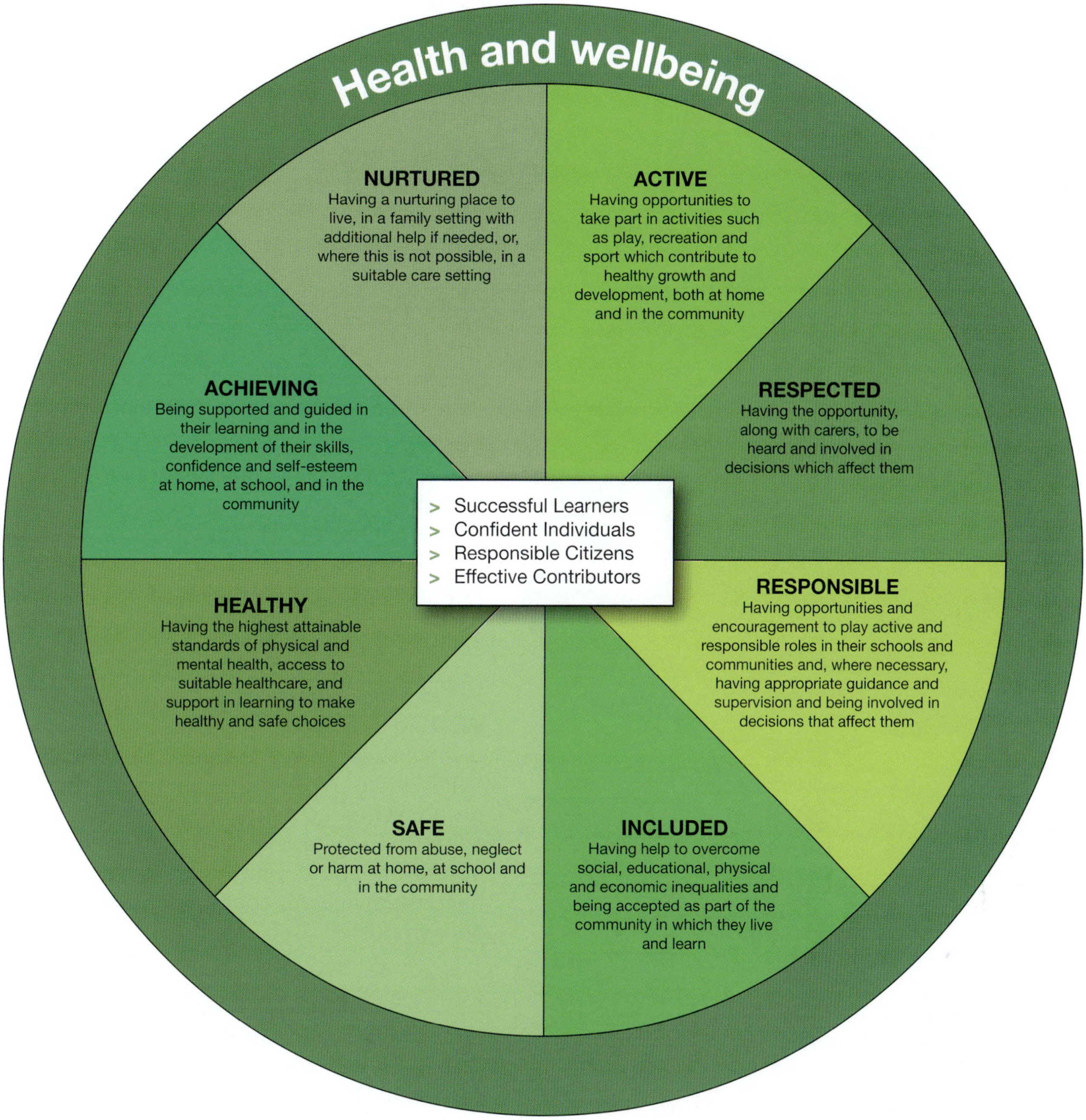

Health and wellbeing

NURTURED
Having a nurturing place to live, in a family setting with additional help if needed, or, where this is not possible, in a suitable care setting

ACTIVE
Having opportunities to take part in activities such as play, recreation and sport which contribute to healthy growth and development, both at home and in the community

ACHIEVING
Being supported and guided in their learning and in the development of their skills, confidence and self-esteem at home, at school, and in the community

RESPECTED
Having the opportunity, along with carers, to be heard and involved in decisions which affect them

> Successful Learners
> Confident Individuals
> Responsible Citizens
> Effective Contributors

HEALTHY
Having the highest attainable standards of physical and mental health, access to suitable healthcare, and support in learning to make healthy and safe choices

RESPONSIBLE
Having opportunities and encouragement to play active and responsible roles in their schools and communities and, where necessary, having appropriate guidance and supervision and being involved in decisions that affect them

SAFE
Protected from abuse, neglect or harm at home, at school and in the community

INCLUDED
Having help to overcome social, educational, physical and economic inequalities and being accepted as part of the community in which they live and learn

Lesson 34 Hey, how are you doing?

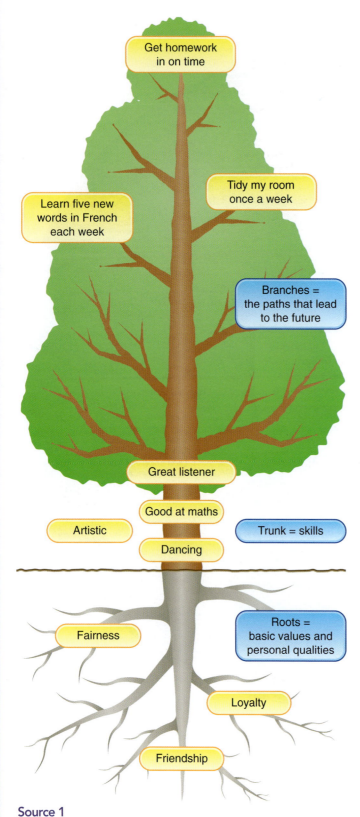

Source 1

Get Active 1

It is really important that children and young people have a big say in the decisions that affect them. This PSHE course has been written to help you learn about your own health and wellbeing.

In your group, look back at the chapter you have been given by your teacher and see if you can agree one key thing that you have learned that was new to all of you.

Get Active 2

The image of the tree in Source 1 depicts a person's good qualities, the skills they have developed, and some of their short-term goals.

You will be given a copy of a tree to complete for yourself. Put your name in the centre of the tree. Think about how you will complete your own tree to symbolise you. Work in a pair and discuss your trees to help each other decide what to put on them.

Get Active 3

Working as a group of six, you will be given a sheet of five leaves to fill in as 'affirmations' of the other members of your group. Write the name of each person on a leaf, then write one thing that you really appreciate about them. Cut them up and hand them in; your contributions will be anonymous.

Get Active 4

Look at the five leaves that have been placed on your tree. Complete this sentence: 'The leaf I appreciate the most is the one that says … because …'

Get Active 5

When you started this PSHE course as a brand new member of First Year you completed a slip of paper that identified at least one step or action you could take towards achieving a goal in your life. Look at that slip of paper and see how far you have gone towards achieving that goal. If you have taken that step, well done! If you haven't managed it yet, don't worry, there's plenty of time.

Index

A
accidents 34–5
achievements 8
addict 22–3
addiction 22–3
alcohol 17, 18, 21, 22, 23
arguments 24–5, 57
assertiveness 66–7

B
budgeting 46–7
bullying 38–9

C
careers 50–1
challenges 68–9
Charter for Young People 7
community services 44
cultural diversity 54–5

D
disagreements 56, 57
drugs 16–23
  media treatment 18–19

E
emergencies 44–5
exercise 13

F
families 24–5
feelings 32–3
Five Main Food Groups 14
food additives 15
friendship 56–7

G
Getting it Right for Every Child (GIRFEC) 70
goals 9, 42–3, 62–3
Goethe, Johann Wolfgang von 62
Group Agreement 6–7

H
healthy eating 14–15
healthy schools 11
hygiene 31

I, J
individuality 54–5
infection control 10–11
interview questions 63

K
keeping clean 31
Khan, Amir 8

L
laws 7, 52
listening 64–5

M, N
money 46–51
NSPCC ambassadors 8

O
Oliver, Jamie 9
online safety 36–7

P, Q
personal development 4–5
personal health 12–13
personal safety online 36–7
positive qualities 60
prescription drugs 21
problem letters 32–3
puberty 30–1, 32–3

R
refusal skills 69

relationships   24–7, 28–9, 56–7
rights and responsibilities   7, 45, 52–3
risk assessment   34–5
risk-taking   20–1
role models   63
rules   52

S
safety online   36–7
savings   47, 48–9
saying no   69
self-esteem   61
SMART targets   43
smoking   17, 21–3
substance misuse 16–23

T
talents   59
target setting   42–3
teamwork   41
teeth   13
tobacco   17, 21
traffic light food labelling system   15

U
United Nations Convention on the Rights of the Child   52–3

V
values   6
Van Gogh, Vincent   59
volatile substances   17, 21

W, X, Y, Z
work   50–1
working with others   40–1

Acknowledgements

The Publishers would like to thank the following for permission to reproduce copyright material:

Photo credits
p.4 *tl* © Profimedia International s.r.o./Alamy, *bl* © wsr/Alamy, *c* © Steven May/Alamy, *tr* © Don B. Stevenson/Alamy, *br* © Dan Atkin/Alamy; **p.8** © Stephen Hird/Reuters/Corbis; **p.9** © Luke MacGregor/Reuters/Corbis; **p.13** *l* © imagebroker/Alamy, *r* © Stephane Cardinale/People Avenue/Corbis; **p.14** Food Standards Agency/eatwell.gov.uk; **p.15** © Alex Segre/Alamy; **p.17** *l* © Bubbles Photolibrary/Alamy, *tr* © Patrick Steel/Alamy, *br* © Harriet Cummings/Alamy, *table l* © Hshen Lim/iStockphoto.com, *table c* © omer sukru goksu/iStockphoto.com, *table r* © Michael Mancini/iStockphoto.com; **p.23** *t* © John Cooper/Alamy, *b* © Awie Badenhorst/Alamy; **p.24** *l* © GoGo Images Corporation/Alamy, *c* Karan Kapoor/Getty Images, *b* © Mango Productions/Corbis, *r* © Chris Carroll/Corbis; **p.26** *l* © Blend Images/Alamy, *c* © GoGo Images Corporation/Alamy, *r* © GoGo Images Corporation/Alamy; **p.27** *t* © Katie Lamb/Alamy, *mt* © Steph Fowler/Brand X/Corbis, *mb* © PhotosIndia.com LLC/Alamy, *b* © Enigma/Alamy; **p.28** *t* © Design Pics Inc./Alamy, *mt* © D. Hurst/Alamy, *mb* © vario images GmbH & Co.KG/Alamy, *b* © Sinibomb Images/Alamy; **p.40** © Timothy Tadder/Corbis RF/ Punchstock; **p.42** Nicola Sutton/Life File; **p.53** Courtesy of the United Nations/Published with permission; **p.54** *tl* © Janine Wiedel Photolibrary/Alamy, *tr* © Cultura/Alamy, *b* © Harry Maynard/Corbis; **pp.54–55** James Woodson/Getty Images; **p.55** *t* © samc/Alamy, *b* © Cultura/Alamy; **p.56** © Scott Hortop/Alamy; **p.67** Eric Audras/Getty Images.

Acknowledgements
p.7 The Scottish Charter , Protecting Children and Young People, www.scotland.gov.uk, 2004, © Crown copyright material is reproduced under Class Licence Number C02P0000060 with the permission of the Controller of HMSO; **p.8** Amir Khan profile, from http://www.amirsfans.co.uk/; **p.9** Jamie Oliver interview, from BBC Newsround http://news.bbc.co.uk/cbbcnews/hi/club/your_reports/newsid_1685000/1685429.stm; **p.19** Scottish Schools Adolescent Lifestyle and Substance Use Survey (SALSUS) National Report 2008, a survey undertaken by Ipsos MORI, commissioned by ISD Scotland on behalf of the Scottish Government, 23 June 2009; **pp.36–37** How To Keep Safe Online adapted from http://news.bbc.co.uk/cbbcnews/hi/find_out/guides/tech/safe_surfing; **p.39** "FIRST DAY AT SCHOOL" by Roger McGough from *In the Glassroom* (© Roger McGough 1976) is printed by permission of United Agents (www.unitedagents.co.uk) on behalf of Roger McGough; extract from the poem 'Pocket Money' is reproduced with the permission of Mick Gowar.

Every effort has been made to trace all copyright holders, but if any have been inadvertently overlooked the Publishers will be pleased to make the necessary arrangements at the first opportunity.

Although every effort has been made to ensure that website addresses are correct at time of going to press, Hodder Gibson cannot be held responsible for the content of any website mentioned in this book. It is sometimes possible to find a relocated web page by typing in the address of the home page for a website in the URL window of your browser.